Praise for

The Downsized Veggie Garden

"IDEAS, that's what this book is all about. If you want the pleasure of a garden, this book will give you plenty of ideas, and you will be amazed at all of the options you really have."

~ *Mel Bartholomew, Creator of the Square Foot Gardening System, author of* All New Square Foot Gardening

"Growing fresh veggies, herbs and fruits can be done in most any space. Kate shares her years of gardening experience to give you the many options for growing the food you enjoy."

~ *Brenda Haas, host of Twitter #gardenchat and co-host of Garden Chatter, HGTVgardens Ask&Share*

"When I first heard that Kate Copsey was writing her own book about growing vegetables, I knew immediately that I wanted a copy. She can dance, you see, and that's what vegetable gardening is all about – a dance involving sun, soil, water, nutrients and a little common sense. Kate gently and confidently guides novices and experts, young and old – even me – through the practical steps necessary to succeed on whatever patch of land or porch or deck or patio we call our 'farm.'"

~ *Mike Nowak, columnist for Chicagoland Gardening magazine, speaker, radio show host, blogger, author of* Attack of the Killer Asparagus

"For baby boomers, newbie gardeners and those who wannabe, having a garden that's just the right size is a must. Too big and you can get discouraged. Too small, and you might be disappointed. Some of us don't have any space for an in-ground garden, so Smart Pots, window boxes and hanging baskets are put to work. With the wisdom that comes from getting her hands dirty, Kate provides the best advice, tips and recommendations to help you succeed in your garden space, from what to grow and when to harvest – all honed to specific regions."

~ *Jo Ellen Meyers Sharp, garden columnist for The Indianapolis Star, contributor to Indiana Gardening, and editor of Iowa Gardener, Michigan Gardening, Minnesota Gardener and Wisconsin Gardening magazines.*

"I wish I had *The Downsized Veggie Garden* when I first started vegetable gardening. It would have saved me time and money and shown me how to grow more food in less space. Kate Copsey is the perfect gardening coach – she's knowledgeable, encouraging, and has a ton of tips and advice on growing and harvesting in small spaces."

> ~ *Niki Jabbour, best-selling author of* Groundbreaking Food Gardens *and* The Year-Round Vegetable Gardener *(2012 Book Award, American Horticultural Society), host of The Weekend Gardener News in Halifax and Ottawa.*

"Kate's book is a timeless reminder and useful guide for new and veteran gardeners alike. Curbing our enthusiasm for over-planting is hugely important – especially when it comes to vegetable gardening. Too much, too soon, can become quickly overwhelming. Kate offers practical ways to grow into our gardens while keeping it fun, productive and manageable."

> ~ *Joe Lamp'l, Executive Producer and host: Growing a Greener World®; Founder and CEO, The joe gardener® Company*

"Kate Copsey must be a kindred spirit, as she finds a place for veggies just about anywhere in the landscape. Didn't think you could have a vegetable garden? Think again! *The Downsized Veggie Garden* is a wonderful addition to any gardener's library. It's packed with great information presented with a friendly voice."

> ~ *Doug Oster, garden columnist for the Pittsburgh Tribune-Review, author of* Tomatoes Garlic Basil

the *downsized*
Veggie Garden

the *downsized*
Veggie Garden

How to Garden Small
Wherever You Live, Whatever Your Space

Kate Copsey

st. lynn's
press

PITTSBURGH

The Downsized Veggie Garden
How to garden small wherever you live, whatever your space

ISBN-13: 978-1-943366-00-2

Library of Congress Control Number: 2015947988
CIP information available upon request

First Edition, 2016

St. Lynn's Press . POB 18680 . Pittsburgh, PA 15236
412.381.9933 . www.stlynnspress.com

Book design – Holly Rosborough
Editor – Catherine Dees

Photo credits:
All photos © Kate Copsey, with the exception of the following:
Holly Rosborough – pgs 1, 9, 35, 39 (top), 40, 48, 49, 51 (bottom), 58, 60, 62, 63, 66, 67, 69, 70, 72, 81, 97, 110, 111, 114 (top), 121, 31, 133, 139 (left), 141, 142, 146, 147, 148;

Asher Wittenberg – pg 12; Carol Case Siracuse and Tom Palamusa – pg 15;

BrazelBerries® – Peach Sorbet Blueberry, pg 114 (right), and Raspberry Shortcake, pg 116;

Matej Kudlicska, Strawberry, pg 11, https://commons.wikimedia.org/wiki/File:Jahoda.jpg;

Amy Gaertner, Winter (Acorn) Squash, pg 150,
https://commons.wikimedia.org/wiki/File:Cucurbita_pepo_Carnival_Acorn_Squash_III.jpg

Printed in China
On certified FSC recycled paper using soy-based inks

This title and all of St. Lynn's Press books may be purchased for educational, business or sales promotional use. For information please write:
Special Markets Department . St. Lynn's Press . POB 18680 . Pittsburgh, PA 15236

10 9 8 7 6 5 4 3 2 1

❧

TO MY PARENTS

AUDREY AND THE LATE MICHAEL WRIGHT

WHO ALWAYS GREW VEGETABLES —
AND EACH WINTER MADE A POTATO TRENCH
WHERE WE DEPOSITED COMPOSTABLE SCRAPS.

❧

Table of Contents

Introduction

This book came out of a discussion with a fellow garden writer, Doug Oster. I was in the middle of relocating from my old home, which had a nice, spacious garden, and was living in a temporary apartment when seed-sowing time came around. I told Doug I couldn't figure out what to sow or where to germinate the seeds, let alone where I was going to grow them! I joked that I needed to write a book on this downsizing thing. Many months and several discussions with Doug later, I approached his publisher, St. Lynn's Press – and here we are. My family did finally move to a permanent home, though much smaller in both square footage and in space to grow vegetables compared to our last home. We are not totally downsized yet, but the lessons learned from that apartment and current challenges in our smaller home – as well as meeting other gardeners who are growing in small spaces – are what this book is all about.

Over the years, we have moved from a simple rental when we first got married to larger properties as the kids came along. It was not until the boys left to make their own lives that we started to go the other way. We didn't need space for the soccer ball to be kicked or the golf ball hit, and we certainly didn't need as many vegetables to feed them. While the boys were growing, I certified as a Master Gardener and became a fan of community gardens that not only feed the community but also bring neighbors together; and I discovered Square Foot Gardening, which made my gardening time so much more productive.

Not everyone travels the same road I did, but I know that growing at least a few vegetables has become a high priority for people of all ages and gardening experience. What might hold someone back is the perception that they need more space than they have available to them. This book is a way to enable all those people who don't want to, or cannot, till-up the "back 40." I'm here to affirm that they have plenty of options for growing in compact spaces and gardens: in-ground (in as little as 16 square feet), in containers, on decks, up walls, on windowsills, and even hydroponically, without soil at all.

The new appreciation of garden-fresh vegetables comes from many sides but includes some health scares in the past decade. Parents want to know where their children's food is coming from and what is put onto that "fresh" vegetable to keep it looking good. When you grow your own veggies you know what they were treated with and when they were harvested. And then there is the rather boring selection found in the local supermarket. People travel to other countries and taste other culinary ingredients only to find that these ingredients are not as readily available back home. Many of those great spices and tasty Italian salad greens can easily be grown in your own small garden.

There is a wealth of great tasting vegetables out there to try, including some that your preteens would turn their nose up at (but maybe not, if they took part in growing them), such as colorful chards, kales and spinach. Now is your chance to enjoy the many colors of tomatoes and other healthy and great tasting vegetables. The trend to growing vegetables in containers and smaller places has led the industry to bring out new cultivars of fruit and vegetables that grow happily in containers. There are even containers that fit snuggly onto a deck railing to optimize your space for seating and entertainment.

If you've spent years tending an extensive vegetable plot to help feed the family like I did, living with a smaller space takes some adjusting to. On the other hand, if your gardening experience has been limited to mowing the lawn and pulling weeds

from the foundation planting, and you'd like to try your hand at growing some vegetables for the first time, this book shows you how you can do that, and in a way that suits your current lifestyle and your current home style.

Whether the home is rented or purchased, an apartment, a house in suburbia or a "mature adult" development, there are many ways that you can grow at least some of your own fruits and vegetables and enjoy the taste of a one-minute-old tomato, raspberry or apple – from right outside your door!

———

I invite you to join me as we walk through the decision-making process for planning and planting your downsized garden. Along the way we'll find the best location for a favorite tomato plant and give you a checklist to make sure the plant will grow there and produce for you. I'll equip you with simple, practical tips to optimize your enjoyment and save time, work and money. And we'll hear from some other downsized gardeners who have found space where they live to grow their own favorite veggies – which in one case meant the roof of a garage!

So whether you are new to vegetable gardening or an old hand – in your first home or your last home – you are exactly where you need to be at this time in your life, and I can promise you some great ideas for successful growing.

Kate

PART ONE

START WHERE YOU ARE

Finding Space to Grow Vegetables Wherever You Live

reative gardeners will always find places to grow things (even rooftops and fire escapes!), but if you are busy commuting from dawn to dusk, your creative juices and gardening time can be very limited. Where you live and the amount of time you can devote to growing even one tomato plant are crucial to vegetable garden success. So our first chapter will look at the very practical issue of deciding what you can grow and where, not to mention how much you want to grow. It all starts with assessing your living space.

Do you live where space for plants is an issue? In small properties like apartments, condos or townhomes, it is possible to grow at least some of your own vegetables. I've done it successfully in my own apartment-living days and quickly learned to make

the most of what I had. When you know *how* your space can be adapted, you will find that you can grow more than you thought.

Small properties are a relative thing, and growing space ranges from an apartment window box to a small backyard. For a larger property, your growing space can be a set of small raised beds placed close to the home, giving you an old-fashioned kitchen garden. Containers can go anywhere but are ideal on decks and patios, as well as porches and balconies. For small backyards, raised beds are perfect.

There is always a play-off between what you want to grow and what you have the room for, as well as the time that you have to care for it. Small plots provide an amazing amount of produce, particularly for a single person or downsizing seniors. However, a family with a couple of teenagers will need more than a few containers to satisfy the appetites of everyone. The trick is to figure out what space you have and start with a few things that you frequently buy from the farm market or supermarket. Some things, like potatoes and raspberries, take up considerably more space per pound of produce than tomatoes or peppers.

But even if you have all the room you need, there is a good case for making just a modest, well planned, productive yet easy to maintain vegetable garden.

Finding Garden Space in Apartments and Condominiums

Most of us have lived in an apartment or condo-minium at some time in our lives. If you are currently living in one and think that it means you can't grow veggies, let's take a look at the possibilities.

Newer Apartments

Apartments can be large, but most are small and compact, often with no outdoor space at all. With the exception of apartments that were created from large, older homes, a modern apartment building is purposely built to optimize space inside and maximize units per building. They are blocky to look at, but usually have plenty of windows. If there is a patio or balcony, it likely comes off the living area and is accessed via a sliding patio door. Access to enough light for growing, either indoors or out, is key.

Orientation and light. South- or west-oriented windows, patios or balconies do best. With windows that face east or north, you are going to need to supplement the natural light – especially if you plan on starting vegetables indoors from seed.

If you are fortunate enough to have a patio on the south side of your building, the options for growing increase significantly because you can "spill" over the edge of the patio; if instead you have a balcony, you'll need to stay within its boundaries.

Apartment rules. Just having the space and orien-tation might not be enough to give you the go-ahead

to garden on a patio or balcony; many new apart-ment complexes rely on uniformity both inside and outside. Hanging baskets from railings or windows might be deemed "untidy." Additionally, if you have a ground floor patio, the landscape crew that sprays weed killers and lawn treatment does not want to run the risk of your consuming contami-nated food – so rules are imposed to ban growing edibles in the ground surrounding the patio, or even on the patio. For this situation, there are some good options for growing indoors, which I'll show you later in the book. But if, for whatever reason, you are not able to grow indoors, I recommend finding a community garden nearby where you can grow your vegetables. I talk about community gardens below.

Older apartment buildings. Older city apartments come in all sizes and configurations, but at the very least, you will always find a window in the main living quarters. True, basement apartments don't admit much light; however, assuming the orientation is favorable, you can grow near these windows. What about windowsills? These can be a bonus in older buildings. If you are willing to move your sofa and mementos to one side, you can create a stable surface on a windowsill for your small containers and plants.

Condominiums and townhomes. Although these are generally larger than apartments, the rules of the development are frequently stringent and can go as far as forbidding any containers on the patio, with the same rationale as the apartment buildings use. The good news is that, regardless of the orientation of the unit, there will most likely be some decent direct sunlight somewhere during the day. And if you have some outside space that allows for small gardens and container planting, you should have good growing options, beyond growing your plants inside.

Dealing with covenants and restrictions. Questions to look at include "Is the outside space common?" If your only personal exterior space is a patio, then placing raised beds on the surrounding grass will not be allowed. But if your unit is organized with dividing panels that delineate at least some outside space for which you are responsible, then you are safe to use it as you please as long as your covenants permit that use. More lenient developments do indeed allow you to use containers and raised beds; others need to be persuaded that the use is within reason. There are even some developments that have their own community gardens.

If you're looking for a condo or townhouse… Taking a walk around different developments will give you an idea of what people are doing, but it is critical to read all the rules before you sign the contract.

A Front Yard Vegetable Garden

Milutin Calukovic was born in the former Yugoslavia. Growing vegetables was something his family had always done. Today, he lives in New Jersey, where his back garden is surrounded with trees and is too shady to grow healthy vegetables. Determined to have a vegetable garden, he turned to the front of the house where there was plenty of sunny space. His first step after site selection was to get some good healthy soil for the plants, which included lots of compost material. The garden occupies the area within the curve of his driveway and has an attractive wood edging. He grows lots of tomatoes, peppers and squash, giving his family plenty for eating fresh and for storing.

Finding Garden Space in Urban and Suburban Homes

Developments from pre-1980 are less likely to have a large book of covenants, whereas gated developments from post-2000 prefer a uniform look for both houses and gardens. Living here can be great, but you do need to know the rules. Many a resident has been taken to task for straying into the realm of "unacceptable under the covenant" and a fence or compost pile has to be removed.

Homes without covenant restrictions. The earlier homes and developments, plus some rural homes, have few if any covenants. Here, you might find gardeners tilling up lawns for vegetables, home-owners growing fruit and vegetables in the front garden, and compost piles in full view of the road.

Styles of urban and suburban houses are as different as the people who live in them. They are usually owner-occupied rather than rented. This leads to a sense of pride in the individual properties as well as the community or neighborhood as a whole – and of course, getting on well with your neighbors is vital for a pleasant and peaceful life. That said, the urge to grow some vegetables has become such a normal part of life today that you will likely find at least some neighbors with a

vegetable garden. Traditionally, these gardens are at the back of the property where raised beds jostle with sand pits and gym sets for space.

A large number of developments are placed on cleared land with ample space to grow both on patios and decks and in the back garden. The downside to the clear view across such developments is that neighborhood cats, dogs, children and deer have a tendency to disregard property lines and trample your young seedlings unless a fence or hedge is placed to deter them. In these neighborhoods, it is conventional to put the vegetables in the back of the property.

Too much shade? But what if you live in a wooded development where the homes are spaced to maximize privacy and enjoyment of nature? Being able to see nature – from birds to deer – is a bonus to wooded lots. The downside is that vegetables do not grow well in wooded areas, and unless there is some cleared space, you will have issues with light. If your wooded area is only at the back and covenants are lenient or nonexistent, the sunny front garden becomes a great place for some vegetables.

Vegetable gardening in your front yard. For a garden in full view of the street, the design and size will be as important as what you grow. Careful

planning and starting gradually will allay any concerns from neighbors. It is also very possible that by growing "out front" – visible to neighbors walking their dogs and mothers taking young children for a stroll – you will find yourself making friends with more people than if your veggie garden is tucked away in the backyard.

There are even more benefits than just fresh produce when you grow your vegetables in the front: It has been said that when one person is seen gardening near the road, a neighbor sees the garden and starts one of his or her own! It is important, of course, that you keep your front yard vegetable garden neat and cared for.

If you'd prefer to be more conventional and have a backyard vegetable garden, but you're prevented because of trees or some other property feature that gives too much shade – here again, the best option may be a community garden. Meeting others from the neighborhood in a community garden allows you to increase the amount you can grow, and also creates a pleasant social environment to grow with other likeminded neighbors.

Older in-town homes. These can offer you some of the most flexibility. You can pretty much do as you please as long as the local township does not have regulations. Wide, sunny porches and pretty picket fences allow for container growing, window boxes, raised beds and in-ground growing. The only criteria to consider are the amount of sun that the proposed vegetable garden will get and keeping the landscape as a whole in tune with the age and style of the property.

Older country homes. Homes along country roads are covenant-free and can come with large acreage. If you are into country living, these are wonderful homes to live in, but unless you are planning to create a self-sufficient homestead, you do not need to till up large areas to grow your vegetables. Small raised beds or gardens make maintenance fast and easy, allowing you the ability to raise some produce while still having the time to enjoy the family and the peaceful area.

Before You Start Your Garden

If you are currently living where you plan to make your downsized vegetable garden – or if you have the luxury of looking for another home that's a perfect fit for the garden you envision – here are a few things to keep in mind. The first and most important is making sure your plants will have the right amount of light.

Follow the sun. Almost all vegetables need some sunshine to thrive. Some vegetables can cope with light shade, but your choices are much broader with at least five hours of sun every day. For heat-loving summer vegetables like tomatoes and peppers, afternoon sun is better than morning sun. Salad greens and winter vegetables can tolerate slightly less sun and grow well with just morning sun in most areas. A very shady balcony, deck or yard is going to be far less productive than a sunny area.

How much sun a location receives changes with the seasons. In mid-summer the angle of the sun to the ground is much higher than in winter.

Consider what can happen when there is a line of trees nearby, or a neighboring building. They might block the low-angled rays of a winter sun, but the high summer sun can clear the tops, making the ground below sunny for summer vegetables. You should also be aware of the types of trees close to the place you plan for your garden. Are they deciduous? A deciduous tree drops its leaves in fall, which allows more sun through in the winter.

If you are evaluating your potential garden space during that time, you could mistakenly think that there will be light enough for your veggies come summer. But when the leaves come out in spring, you could be unpleasantly surprised to find the trees are blocking the sunlight, so a spot that was sunny in winter is now too shady to grow summer vegetables.

East-west is best. If you are house- or apartment-hunting, you will ideally want to see the location in summer so that you can assess the sunlight, but a general guide would be to find a home with an east-west orientation. Having morning sunlight streaming into kitchen windows and afternoon sun bathing your balconies and patios gives you optimum possibilities for your garden plans. On the other hand, a north-south orientation gives very little direct sun in the morning and afternoon. Likewise, an apartment unit on the north side of a building would be problematic for growing vegetables.

Having sun coming directly through a sunny window is particularly important for indoor growing, as well as for starting seeds. A room that is light enough for most people is generally not sufficiently bright for vegetables to thrive. The intensity of light decreases rapidly from a window to the center of a room. Modern window glazing impedes the rays coming in from the sun just as it keeps drafts and cold temperatures out of the room. Consequently, an apparently bright, sunny room that is lit by indirect sunlight may be pleasant to sit

in and perfectly fine for many houseplants, but it is not bright enough for many vegetables, such as summer squash or eggplants.

Unless you have a bright, south-facing room with lots of window space, some supplemental light will be essential for indoor growing.

Apartment Growing

Asher Wittenberg is a young man starting his professional life in New York City, where he has an apartment. He enjoys cooking but found that essential fresh herbs were hard to find and expensive to buy. His mother, garden writer Nan Sterman, sent Asher some seeds so that he could grow fresh herbs on his sunny windowsill. The container is placed outside the window on a ledge that is about 8 inches deep, and he waters the garden by opening the window next to the garden. Now Asher is enjoying his first garden and harvesting fresh lettuce as well as basil and cilantro for his recipes.

Basil, cilantro and colorful lettuce fill the container.

This container of herbs sits comfortably on a ledge outside Asher's window.

Water. For healthy growth, plants need consistent water. Since nature does not always provide that, the gardener will have to supplement where necessary. Outside containers are particularly hungry for water and dry out very quickly in the height of summer (see page 40 for container watering solutions). It goes without saying that an outside spigot is very helpful for watering both containers and the garden plot. Don't place your garden area too far from the water source, because two or three hoses strung together produces a much lower stream of water than just a single hose. Think about getting one of the modern hoses that coil or roll into small bundles for neat storage; they take up much less space than a conventional hose. A timer on the hose to water at dawn is also useful but can be wasteful if the water comes on during a rainstorm, so keep an eye on the weather forecast and adjust the timer when necessary. Too much water can be as detrimental to a plant as too little.

Sharing space with your vegetables. Your vegetable garden might end up competing for space with other things, like gym sets, sand pits and paddling pools – or a volleyball net and room to throw a soccer ball. For balconies and patios, you need to leave room for a chair or two and maybe a barbecue. Your enthusiasm for colorful, productive containers can be wonderful until the sheer number of containers makes it hard for you to turn around! **Finding balance.** The reality is that you probably will not be able (or willing) to grow every vegetable you like to eat – whether you don't have the time, energy or space, or you love some vegetables that take up too much room for a small home plot. I recommend growing some things at home, some things in a community garden, then using a farm stand or farmer's market to supplement your homegrown produce. That way, you are optimizing your garden space. And don't forget the value of exchanging garden produce with friends who also garden.

Rooftop Gardening

There has been a revolution in growing vegetables in less conventional spaces, and that includes rooftops. For a simple container, this is not a big deal as long as you can get water to the garden. More extensive rooftop gardens require careful planning and more than likely require permission as well. For apartment dwellers though, this can be a wonderful space to have a small garden – with abundant sunshine and no animals to create havoc when the crops are ripe (except for fruit-loving birds). Definitely worth looking into!

A Garage Does Double Duty

Carol Siracuse and Tom Palamusa live on a small urban plot that has neither sun nor room in the front or back to successfully grow all the vegetables that they wanted to use. Their solution was to create a garden on the roof of their garage. It is accessed with a library ladder and affectionately known as the vegetable library. In the three years since they started, the garden has expanded to 20 wooden boxes lined up along the supporting edge of the garage roof. The garden is watered primarily with a hose. Because the garage faces the driveway and road, Carol and Tom incorporate colorful flowers in among the vegetables.

Gaining Space by Vertical Growing

Vertical growing has been around as long as container growing. You have probably seen espaliered fruit trees in walled gardens or grape vines in greenhouses – both using the vertical plane to allow the tree or vine to grow in a protected environment. (Espalier is an ancient method of artistically pruning branches against a frame or wall to control growth.) More recently, though, the idea of using that vertical plane to grow vegetables, or to maximize the space on a patio, has taken on a new look. Tomatoes,

which traditionally have been grown from the ground up and supported on stakes, continued that way until the "upside down" tomato bag came along, which strung the tomato on a support and let the plant grow down toward you for harvesting. If you like the idea of growing strawberries, they don't always have to be in a strawberry pot – or even a space-saving pot, like the one shown here; they can be planted in a hanging basket or other non-traditional vertical container to free up more ground space for conventional containers. The same can be done with herbs.

Vining plants. Vining plants such as peas, beans, squash and melons also use the vertical plane, but will need to be supported. Besides conventional supports and cages, deck or balcony railings do just as fine a job. A bonus to vining plants is that you can grow them on a trellis to create a temporary privacy fence when you are living close to your neighbors.

Vertical growing systems. The trend toward growing vegetables on patios and balconies has spurred the industry to develop not just small-growing varieties but also vertical growing systems that will support several containers, one above the other.

Combining all these ideas provides a way to maximize the square footage of growing space while minimizing the square footage on the ground.

Square Foot Gardening

Back in 1981, retired engineer Mel Bartholomew revolutionized the home vegetable garden with his book *Square Foot Gardening*. His idea was that home vegetable gardening was not just a scaled-down version of farming and the guidelines for farming were not necessarily appropriate for the home gardener. Prior to his method of gardening, we were all encouraged to till up, clear stones from the area, rake flat then sow a 10-foot row of cabbage seed. When the cabbage seed germinated, we took most of the seedlings out so that the remaining cabbages could grow at one foot apart.

Square Foot Gardening disregards this wasteful idea and says that if you want five cabbages, you sow five seeds, each at one foot apart in a grid system. Most seed available to home gardeners has a very high germination rate, so each of the five cabbages is very likely to germinate and produce a great head of cabbage for your kitchen. When combined with a 4-foot-square garden space, Square Foot Gardening creates 16 one-foot cells.

Here's an example of what you can fit into those 16 cells in a 4-foot square:

4 tomato plants	32 carrots
2 peppers	24 lettuces
18 onions	

The Square Foot Gardening system was maybe a little before its time, but in the last decade the popularity of community gardens has made this simple system a standard way of gardening. You can continue adding these 4x4 modules as you have the room and energy to cultivate them. The system also encourages you to fix the grid onto the bed. You will find many community gardens with the grids in place throughout the growing season. After a year or two, you will be able to gauge the grid spacing without a grid, but it does stop over-planting, particularly if you are new to gardening.

Raised Beds. Raised beds work well with the Square Foot Garden philosophy for gardeners who prefer not to till. Whether your native soil is sand or clay, the raised bed will provide the best fertile environment for the plants. The advantage of the raised bed is that you fill it with a soil mix that is weed-free and very loose, which makes it perfect for roots to grow quickly, and easy to pull the odd weed out. Most raised beds are 4-10 inches deep – the greater depth being preferred for growing root crops such as carrots and potatoes. Your local lumber dealer will usually have 4, 6, 8, or 10-inch boards. (Smaller kits of 4x4-foot beds are generally 4-6 inches in depth.) See Chapter Two for lots more about raised beds.

Community Gardens

The interest in growing vegetables has also led to an increase in the number of community gardens with plots available for the local residents. Some require that you reside within the city limits; others are sited in enclosed communities with gardens just for the residents. A typical plot is about 4 feet wide and 8-10 feet in length. Combine these gardens with the Square Foot method of layout, and you can obtain a sizeable harvest that saves hundreds of dollars a year in fresh produce. Community gardens attract a cross section of the community, with a range of ages and backgrounds. They are a wonderful way to get to know other gardeners in your area and chat about different vegetables that you grow – and maybe swap some fresh produce as well. When gardeners of various ethnic origins grow vegetables from their homeland it benefits not only their family but also the other gardeners, who learn about a new vegetable, how it tastes and how to use it. This is a movement that is good for everyone involved.

Visit the American Community Garden Association (https://communitygarden.org/) to find a garden near you.

A Word about Farmers' Markets and Community Supported Agriculture

Once you are growing a few of your own vegetables, you will start to notice that the freshness and flavor of the warm, just-picked tomato or melon is markedly different from the store-bought varieties. Of course, you cannot grow the whole of your weekly vegetables in a window box, but growing some at home and supplementing with a weekly visit to the farmers' market is an excellent option. Just like community gardens, we have seen a sharp increase in the number of farm markets springing up in most suburban and even urban areas. The markets can be year-round or seasonal and the rules for selling

It's important to know how the produce is grown. Talking to the farmers will alert you to whether they are growing organically, naturally or using conventional chemical treatments. Most farmers are happy to share their methods with you, particularly if they are growing with as few chemicals as possible.

One popular way to make sure you get great fresh vegetables all through the summer regardless of what you grow is to enroll in a CSA (Community Supported Agriculture). A CSA farm grows a variety of mixed vegetables through the season and sells shares to the public. The share, or half share, is paid for in advance, and in return the farmer provides a box of produce each week for the shareholder. The shares can also include locally baked breads, eggs and meat. The share can be ready for pick-up at the farm or delivered to a convenient central location. Some farmers prefer to distribute the share boxes at the farm market.

vary from market to market. The first major crop to ripen in the fields is strawberries, marking the starting point for most seasonal markets – April in warmer areas to late May in colder regions. The end of the season brings us sweet corn and pumpkins and marks the closing of the seasonal markets – September or October for most locations.

Most of the vendors at the markets are the farmers who grow the produce. The variety of produce available from specialty vendors is amazing. If you enjoy heirloom beans or tomatoes, you are likely to find a farmer who also likes them too. And they are happy to share recipes and cooking tips, as well as growing tips if you are trying to grow some at home. Region-wide issues such damp, cool weather that delays or destroys your crop would also hit the local farmers, so talking to them about how they deal with the problems can be a big help.

CSA organizations allow the small farmer to fund and plan his or her growing season, knowing that they have a market for the produce. When unusual crops are included in the share, most will give recipes to help you use them. Many have Facebook pages and websites where you can see what is in this week's share. Or chat with others who are part of the same CSA and find out what they made with the produce. Open days at the farm are also advertised so that you can see the farm working and celebrate the season with your own farmer. ∎

Designing a Vegetable Garden that Works for You
(All About Raised Beds and Containers)

*W*hen our eldest and his new wife purchased their first home, we went down to Atlanta to visit them. He took me into the fenced back yard and asked if they could put a small garden somewhere and maybe some herbs. The whole area was bathed in full sun and currently had only lawn with a small foundation bed. Two hours later we had shopped for supplies, assembled this 4x4 kit and and created not just a raised bed filled with colorful lettuce, but also a little herb garden right outside the back door where it is easy to reach. For new gardeners, such an almost instant garden is a perfect place to start.

The "ideal" vegetable garden is the one that fits into your lifestyle, your available space and how it connects with your home activities. What is the

best way to evaluate your available space and needs? I recommend making a sketch of your property; it doesn't have to look professional. A good way to begin your design is to draw the area on a piece of squared or graph paper and mark both the hardscape and vegetation areas.

Hardscape is the part of the landscape that is manmade, including areas that cannot be tilled. Any area covered with concrete or gravel is considered to be hardscape. Mark things like the driveway, fencing, deck or patio – things that can't be moved or changed. Gravel paths can be moved if necessary, but if they are in a logical position such as a line to the garden shed, they are probably counted as hardscape too.

A typical landscape design takes into consideration the utility areas, such as where the garbage/recycle boxes go, compost areas, and entertainment areas that are currently in place. Also, mark lawns and existing tilled areas and trees. For a patio or deck, be sure to note seating and other amenities you plan to keep. When the overall layout of the property is on paper, the fun begins: where to put the vegetables and how many should I grow?

With so many demands on space, it is often difficult to define just one area for the vegetables. So rather than trying to find one garden space for all your vegetables, try finding areas that can double for more than one use. A small container with lettuce or herbs is quite happy on the deck – but will also be fine in the center of a patio table where your guests can snip a few leaves to put into their sandwich right where they are eating! Likewise, window boxes look lovely on the deck railings when filled with flowering annuals, but if you slip in a colorful pepper or tomato, you create a mixed container that looks attractive as well as being productive.

Vegetables are plants too! Sometimes we get hung up on finding a perfect place for the vegetables and forget that they are just plants. A vegetable can be an annual, perennial or even a shrub. Just as an attractive ornamental shrub looks fine in the garden, so can an edible shrub such as blueberries. An integrated landscape mixes up all the garden plants, both vegetables and ornamentals: lettuce in the rose garden, tomatoes along the fence line in front of

clematis and a row of blue kale used as a border to the perennial bed. This integration is particularly important if you want to grow your vegetables in the front garden where curb appeal is expected. See how nice those colorful chives look on the page opposite.

Or, the area for your vegetables can be placed as a stand-alone raised bed. For an apartment or condo with a deck or hardscaped patio, you can design with interesting containers, as well as vertical treatments. Much more about containers below, but first let's look at raised beds.

6 Great Vegetables for the Front Garden:

Our front gardens are on show to the world, so having attractive looking vegetables is important. Try these colorful vegetables in your sunny front yard garden.

Artichoke: This is a large back-of-the-border plant with great yellow flowers.

Red basils: Red or purple basils make great foliage plants at the start of the summer, and then the pink flowers turn it from foliage to a beautiful flowering annual.

Chards: No longer are chards basic green with white stems, they now come with bright red or yellow stems and make great middle-of-the-border plants.

Kales: Kales can be blue or green, large or small. Try the curly blue kales for a border in front of your perennial bed, or the large kale in front of an evergreen hedge.

Red pepper: Small, bright red jalapeno peppers brighten up the middle of any garden.

Okra: A common Southern annual that can be grown everywhere, the okra plants put out hibiscus-like flowers in white or red. They are one of the most attractive vegetables and grow to about 4 feet, so place at the back or middle of the garden bed.

Raised Beds

Raised beds are a perfect solution for many situations in the garden, like poor soil or hardscape that makes digging in the garden impossible. Raised beds can also be looked at as a temporary solution in rental properties, as you can disassemble them almost as easily as you can make them. One of the many advantages to a raised bed is the ease of maintenance. The loose, soilless mix is free of weeds and grass at the start, and any weeds that arrive are easy to remove. Most beds can be weeded in a matter of minutes.

Don't get hung up on size! Although most plans for raised beds refer to a 4x4-foot square bed, it is not the only dimension you can use. Maybe your small area can't accommodate a 4-foot width but is longer than 4 feet, such as along a wall or building. A 2x8-foot bed works just as well as a square one. The minimum dimension for one large vegetable plant – say, a tomato or cabbage – is a 1x1-foot square, so you're free to think in terms of several squares all together – or you can slot the vegetables around the garden, using one square foot here and another one somewhere else. That one square foot is also big enough for many little mesclun and salad plants and almost a dozen onions, scallions and leeks.

Building a Raised Bed

Raised beds in a community garden.

Materials to Frame the Bed

The gardens are going to be outside, so consider weather resistance in the materials you select. You can buy complete raised bed kits, including the boards, corners and anchors all in one box. You will probably need a Phillips-head screwdriver to screw the corner pieces in and a mallet or hammer to drive the anchors into the ground. The downside to most commercial kits is the depth of bed – most are 6 inches deep, a minimum for healthy roots, but some kits are only 4 inches in depth, which is a little shallow for many vegetables.

Here are some things to know about the materials, whether you choose a kit or build your own bed from scratch:

■ *Cedar:* Cedar is a naturally long-lasting material that needs no added sprays to make it weatherproof – and it looks great in the garden, which is why most commonly available kits use cedar boards that will last for many seasons. Box store lumber departments and lumber merchants usually have cedar boards. The only decision to make when buying the lumber is how deep you want the bed. Standard boards come in 6, 8 or 10-inch widths and lumber departments have 8, 10 or 12-foot lengths. Most stores will cut the boards to 4 feet, which is a standard size for beds and fits easily into cars.

■ *Redwood:* Redwood has similar insect and moisture resistance as cedar and makes an excellent raised bed frame. The weathered redwood boards take on an attractive gray color that blends nicely into any landscape. Alas, redwood raised bed kits or boards are not always as easy to find as cedar.

■ *Composite materials:* These materials are similar to those used on decks. Composites are a blend of polymers and wood, giving a natural wood look and feel but with greater weather resistance. Kits made from composite material are found at many large stores, but you could have trouble finding boards to make your own beds.

■ *Recycled plastic:* Garden beds, edging and raised bed kits made from weather resistant recycled plastic are very common. Costs vary tremendously, though you do get lots of color options, from bright primary colors to more subtle cedar colors, redwood colors and browns. The materials are generally lightweight compared to cedar beds and are a great option for temporary beds.

■ *Non-wood beds:* There is no rule that a raised bed has to be made from wood-like boards – it can be constructed with breeze blocks, bricks and almost anything that can keep the soil inside from flowing out. Concrete blocks are economical to buy and very easy to assemble, and though not particularly attractive in the beginning, they are quite acceptable when filled with vegetables and flowers.

What size do you need? Raised beds can, of course, be of any size you like, but most commercial kits are for 4x4-foot beds. These can be placed one on top of the other to make deeper beds or extended to make an 8x4-foot bed. Depths vary from 4-6 inches in the smaller sets to a full 8 inches in larger sets. For the first year, a simple 4x4 is probably a good way to go. Buying the lumber and getting it cut to size is often cheaper than buying sets, unless

Not all raised beds need wood – concrete blocks and bricks work well too.

you get last year's kit on sale in late winter. If you opt for building the garden yourself, you can pick the depth that suits you. For root vegetables such as carrots and potatoes, 10 inches is the minimum depth for successful growth.

■ *Width:* A 4-foot width is the most common bed size because most people can reach about 2 feet inside a bed, so from either side, anything within that 4-foot bed can be tended to. The material inside a raised bed is very friable (light and easy for roots to penetrate) and loose and is quickly compacted when walked on, so tending the beds from the edge is an important consideration. And because the 4-foot width is standard, most added screens and hoops are made to fit a 4-foot frame. This does not mean that you can't make the bed 3 feet or even 2 feet in width if that is better for your space.

■ *Length:* It is totally up to you. A 4-foot square is a good starting point, but if you really like row crops such as peas and beans, you could consider a longer bed, maybe 8 or even 10 feet. This is particularly useful when you want to rotate what grows in the garden next year (see page 58 for tips on crop rotation).

■ *Corners and anchors:* Kits come complete with corner anchors, screws and brackets, items that will need to be purchased if you plan to build the bed yourself. There are a few different ways to anchor the boards together, and some are easier than others.

A raised planter with adjustable wheels (with brakes) allows a gardener to stand or sit while tending to the plants.

Adaptive Gardening: Many people who find it difficult to stand or who are restricted to a wheel-chair can still enjoy gardening – not only by using the edge of a raised bed as a seating platform, but by raising the whole garden bed on legs to achieve a comfortable height. Here's how:

Using the same 4x4-foot design, construct a raised bed from wood as normal. Then fix a base to the bed and secure it. The base can be wood boards or a 4x4 sheet of sturdy wallboards. The boards should be weather resistant and able to not only support the weight of wet soil but allow drainage as well, so drill a few holes into a board to allow the water to drain easily. Finally, attach the legs on each corner at the correct height for the gardener who should be able to reach to about the middle of the bed. An alternate design is to make the depth of the whole garden bed about 2 feet and create a broader seating area around the perimeter (8-12 inches), so that a person with limited mobility can sit down comfortably and easily reach into the bed to tend the plants. See page 34 for a word about adaptive tools.

Fill that Raised Bed!

You have found a place for the raised bed in the sun and constructed the bed – and now it is time to fill the bed with healthy growing medium. **Do not** use regular garden soil taken from a nearby garden bed, as that soil is dense and filled with bacteria and contaminants. In fact, the clay or sand that you have in the garden is one of the reasons people resort to the raised bed in the first place, so nothing is achieved by filling the bed with that soil. A preferred mix is a combination of compost plus aerators. Garden centers carry a variety of suitable growing mediums. Composts from cows or mushrooms sit alongside container mixes and organic mixes. Readymade mixes come complete with a light texture and frequently a fertilizer too. For vegetables, it is best to look for a mix that either has an organic label or does not include urea fertilizer.

A perfect mix can be made right next to the raised bed and includes material from a variety of bags, each containing a slightly different set of nutrients.

Compost should be the dominant part of your mix and this can be from single or multiple sources. Next, you'll add some perlite. Perlite is a volcanic material that helps to lighten the soil, aerate and increase drainage to the overall mix. Finally, add peat moss. The overall mix should end up being about 50% compost, 30% peat moss and 20% perlite. These do not have to be exact, but follow this general guide.

For a single raised bed, empty a few of the bags into the bed and mix the contents together, then add another bag and mix that in. This way you get an even mix throughout the whole bed. If you are doing multiple raised beds it is easier to mix the ingredients on a tarp next to the beds and use a small snow shovel to mix it.

How much mix do I need for the size of my bed?

A 4x4-foot bed that is 8 inches deep has a volume of 9.5 cubic feet. Here is how the 50/30/20 ratio works for that size bed:

50% COMPOST
The average small bag of compost is about 1.5 cubic feet, so you need 3.25 cubic feet of compost or about 3 bags.

30% PEAT MOSS
It comes in bales that expand when damp; a small bale yields about 3 cubic feet.

20% PERLITE
It comes in small or large bags, the smaller ones being about 1.5 cubic feet.

50% compost / 3.25 cu ft.	1.5 cu ft. per bag	3 bags
30% peat moss / 3 cu ft.	3 cu ft. per bale	1 small bale
20% perlite / 1.9 cu ft.	1.5 cu ft. per bag	1 small bag

Tools to Make Things Easier

Not all gardeners are the same size or have the same mobility. For instance, women generally have smaller hands compared to men, but a lot of things can affect the ability of a gardener to grip well or bend over. Just as small children need special tools to help them work comfortably in the garden, so do seniors and those with medical issues that reduce the strength of a person's grip. As the population overall has matured, the industry has started to address these issues and come out with ergonomic tools to make tilling and planting a little easier for us all.

Tools for kids: If you are going to spend time messing with plants, it is only natural that your children will want to help. This can be a healthy activity for them and using the right tools will help them feel productive. Look for small-radius hand tools, and if possible, check the grip while still in the store. Metal tools are better than plastic. A basic child's set of tools will consist of a metal trowel to plant and a pair of clippers to harvest peppers or other produce that cannot be easily picked from the vine.

Tools for adults: For making a new raised bed, you will need to have a full-sized digging fork to turn over the soil in the bed each year. Also, be sure to have a spade for adding new compost and a rake to smooth out the garden before sowing seeds or planting out your seedlings. Before you purchase the spade at the store, make sure its size works for you. Check to see if your arms are at a comfortable

height to be able to dig down into the soil. Although there are not too many options in sizes, there are some slightly smaller-handled spades, particularly useful if you are petite. And finally, you will need a trowel and clippers to plant seedlings and harvest.

Tools with grip adaptions: There are great tools available now for those who have wrist issues and/ or poor grips or who want to avoid getting those problems. Ergonomically curved hand tools relieve stress on the wrist by allowing a straighter angle for digging. Right-angled hand tools make for easier holding as you dig or rake.

Care of tools: Unless you are digging in heavy clay soil on a wet day, your tools will likely not get too dirty, but you should keep them dirt-free. A quick wipe down with a damp cloth or lightly oiled cloth will keep them in order. At the end of the season, some 3-in-1-type machine oil will keep them clean for storage, particularly those with moving parts like clippers. Diseases are easily spread from one area of the garden to another, so always wipe the tools with rubbing alcohol when dealing with diseased plants.

Container Basics

Containers can add beauty and flexibility to your garden space. They can be decorative focal points to accent your home or an area of the garden, or they can be purely utilitarian where the primary consideration is for a vessel to grow vegetables. Most containers fall somewhere in the middle, and cost can certainly be a major element in deciding which type to use. Remember that the plants really don't care what the container is so long as it drains well! (For a review of the many types of containers available today, their advantages and drawbacks, see page 161.)

A Little History

Growing in containers is not new – the ancient Egyptians, Greeks and Romans all used containers to grow trees and ornamental plants, particularly around temples. The Renaissance gardener grew ornamental flowers in containers as well. By the Victorian era, we saw ferns, indoor containers and orangeries installed by the gentry to house tender plants in winter, such as citrus plants and grape vines. The majority of container growing in the twentieth century, particularly the last third of the century, was purely ornamental.

Then the movement to grow your own vegetables began and the whole idea of growing at least some vegetables in containers took off. The plant industry responded by developing new breeds of vegetables that were small enough to be grown in containers, allowing more people to join the movement and enjoy homegrown fruit and vegetables.

A Comfortable Way to Garden

Camille De Santis is an older gardener who prefers to garden in containers that are easy to look after and produce plenty for her needs. She finds it hard to tend to a garden that requires kneeling. Her property is open to the neighbors, so she mixes containers with vegetables alongside containers with flowers to create a productive and attractive patio area. Her crop includes herbs for cooking in the summer and lots of tomatoes for fresh salads and canning. She has a mix of containers – a few large ones set on the ground, two Earthboxes that have wheels on them and two garden boxes that are raised to hip height for ease of care. With these containers, she can enjoy gardening without the discomfort of tending a garden bed.

Containers can be almost any size and shape and made of many different materials – but in general, they can be divided into two groups: those that are meant to be used for growing plants in and those that are meant to be attractive focal points on the deck, patio or garden. The big difference between these two groups is a drainage hole at the bottom. Decorative outer pots are often used to cover and conceal the growing container, such as a pretty window box that holds three or four herbs, each in its own nursery container. The hole at the base of each black nursery pot allows water to drain out – particularly important for outdoor containers, which are subject to downpours of rain in addition to the water that you supply.

Drainage. Containers that do not have a hole in the base create a pond of water under the plants, and therefore the roots cannot get much-needed air. Even though roots are underground, they rely on tiny gaps in the soil structure to access oxygen and to allow the roots to grow through as well as to draw nutrients into the plant.

Same plastic container used for spring bulbs and summer veggies.

There are some containers, mostly plastic ones, that do not come with the hole in the base, but that have small areas you can punch through for drainage. Drainage holes in other containers can be made by taking a screwdriver to the upturned container and hitting it with a mallet or hammer. This works very well with recycled garden trugs that may have broken handles but are too good to throw out. Make several small holes in the base of these cheap containers for drainage, fill with potting mix and plant them with spring bulbs and healthy vegetables!

You can also find containers made of naturally porous material, such as hay basket designs lined with natural coco liners – or the newer fabrics.

For containers that allow drainage, you need to think about where the water is draining to – if you have a group of containers on an apartment balcony that frequently drips muddy water off the balcony onto the residents underneath, you will not be popular! In this situation, your growing container should be placed inside an attractive cover container to catch the excess water. A lipped tray under containers also helps to catch drips.

How big is that container?

The landscape industry has devised its own way of referring to growing containers. Small nursery pots are labeled by the inch, measured diagonally, and larger shrubs are sold by the gallon. Ornamental containers are usually circular and measured by diameter.

Lightening the load: Larger containers, particularly ceramic containers, are heavy even without the growing mix inside, so it is best to place the container in its final position before filling with potting mix and watering. These larger containers, though, are quite deep, and most vegetables do not need that depth to be productive. One way to lighten the whole container is to fill the lower half with empty soda cans or milk cartons.

Plastic inserts are also available that fit snugly into the container at about halfway down. The shelf supports the soil mix above the insert while also allowing water to drain out of the mix and reducing the overall weight of the container.

Where is the light? Whatever your container, it should be placed where there is lots of light. The exception to this is possibly the South, Southwest and far West where some vegetables like salad greens, and herbs like mint and lemon balm, wilt badly in hot afternoon summer sun. Most of the

A plastic shelf insert raises the bottom of the container – with this method you don't need as much soil as you would without it.

Here's one example of a self-watering container. Note the tube where water goes in.

Some plants require more moisture than others, and the amount of watering you have to do will depend on where you live and the container itself – smaller containers take more watering than larger ones. Just as important is the consistency of the water supply. Tomatoes particularly are very susceptible to blossom end rot, which occurs when the moisture level is not consistent. If your container is outdoors, some variation in moisture will occur from rain showers and storms, so be vigilant and check the level of moisture frequently. In dry spells, the plants may need to be watered twice a day. Try to water early in the day and aim for the soil surface rather than the leaves of the plant.

vegetables are fine in an open area, but they do need to be watered more frequently, particularly on hot, sunny days. Containers that are placed with a light shade in the late afternoon will do fine in most areas. Northern growers, where the sun is not as hot, are best to allow the container to be in as much sun as possible. For seedlings, a little more shade is needed too; they can wilt in hot sun, so keep a light cover over the container until the seedlings are well settled and strong enough to survive direct rays from the sun.

Where is the water? After full sun, a vegetable garden needs ample water and good drainage.

Self-watering containers: Watering plants on a regular basis can be an issue in our busy lives. This is where self-watering containers can help. With self-watering containers, the water is held in a reservoir at the bottom – the growing medium and the plants being in the top half. The amount of water the plants need is readily available. For the person who is out all day or away for the weekend and cannot water a container once, let alone twice, every day, this is perfect. Simply add a jug of water to the container's reservoir every few days, at a time you

choose, and you will keep both the plants and your schedule happy.

Drip Irrigation: Most overhead sprinklers and soaker hoses are not convenient to use for containers. Consider using a drip hose. This is particularly useful for a balcony where you have several containers that all need watering. The drip hose is a solid flexible hose that carries the water to the plants. A cut is made where the hose extends across the container, and a T-junction inserted, which allows a small side pipe to divert water to the plant. A small nozzle lets water seep directly to the root zone. Installing these junctions, tributaries and nozzles will supply water to each container and plant efficiently, so you can water everything at one time. Add a timer to the exterior water faucet and your plants will be watered before you get up in the morning or any time.

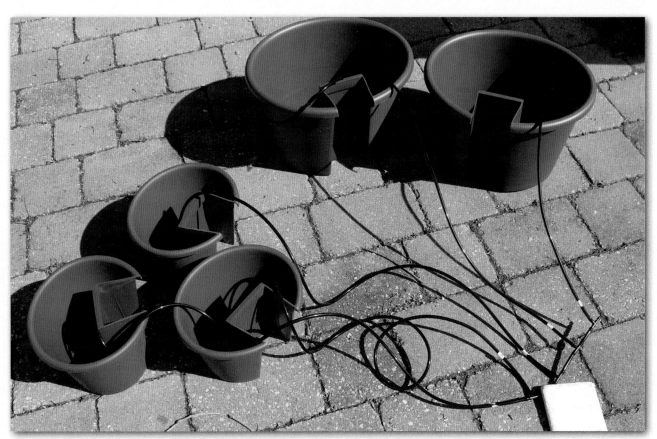

This drip irrigation system will be used in these vertical stacking containers once they're planted with veggies (see photo and information about vertical stacking on page 91).

Container Design Tip: For the most part, the design of the container for growing vegetables is secondary to what you want to grow, but it's worth noting a few tips to make the plants happy and the container attractive. Floral designers look for three sorts of plants for an aesthetic container design: the tall "thriller," the midsize "filler," and the cascading "spiller." Additionally, they look for balance in the container where 1/3 of the height is the container and 2/3 is plant material. For example, in a container that is 24 inches in height: it could use a tall tomato in the middle as the thriller, a ring of burgundy basil as the filler and some container-sized zucchini draping over the sides.

Along with the aesthetic design, it is important that you remember not to shade out smaller varieties that need sunlight. So keep the container of tall beans behind the container of peppers, and the less-tall peppers will thank you!

With a little planning there is a garden design that is right for you. Whether you are in cramped, temporary quarters or have room for lots of gardens but no time to attend them, you can still grow some of your own healthy vegetables. ▪

THREE

Let's Get Growing!
(Seed Starting, Fertilizing and Healthy Soil)

There are two ways you can grow your vegetables – from small starter plants you buy at the nursery, or from seed. Either way will give you your veggies. So why grow from seed? Two main reasons are price and selection. A packet of seed is a few dollars and contains anything from a dozen large melon seeds to a hundred or more tiny lettuce seeds. The number of seeds in a single packet will usually be sufficient for a decent crop. Seeds are also readily available everywhere, from garden centers, hardware stores and online. Starter plants from the nursery are many times more expensive. Admittedly, they allow instant gratification, so I'm not saying not to buy starter plants. But there are some vegetables that do not come as starter plants and you will have to grow from seed. This includes root crops such as carrots, and traditional row crops like beans and peas.

Scarlet runner beans – these are started from seed.

43

Seeds vs. Starter Plants

SEEDS	STARTER PLANTS
Many seeds per packet	1 large plant or 6 small seedlings per container
Cheap to buy	Cost more
Better selection	Limited selection
Too many seeds per packet	Just buy the number you need
Take time to grow	Can be put directly into the ground
Row crops and root crops: Yes	No: Plants not available at nurseries

When is growing from seed not as cost effective? In general, if you want a lot of plants, such as a dozen or more basil or lettuce plants, then it is better to grow from seed. However, if you only want one or two tomato plants or one rosemary plant, then it is better to buy the plant.

Growing from Seed

Seeds are often started indoors to get a jumpstart on the season. This is not always needed, though; cool weather crops like lettuce, kale, carrots, peas and squash will grow and mature just as well when planted directly outdoors ("direct sown") as they will in a seedling container.

Tips for sowing seeds directly in the ground:

- Always check for the last frost date in your area before sowing the seeds.

- Carrots and peas can be sown before the last frost date, whereas squash seeds need to wait a week or two longer.

- Beans can be sown up to two weeks before the last frost and will grow in cool soil – but you could lose the new seedlings if you get a frosty night.

- Keep all the direct sown seeds moist until they have germinated and are growing well.

- Lettuce, kales and chards can be started indoors for an early crop, and then sown directly into the ground or container for a main season crop.

- Tomatoes can also be direct sown into the garden but they will not mature and produce fruit in short-summer areas, so either buying the plant or starting indoors is a much better option.

Peas are direct sown from seed.

Whether you are planning to start your seeds indoors or direct sow outdoors, here are some seed basics you should know.

"What do I want to grow?" Choices, choices...

The seed catalogues, both physical and online, contain an unbelievable number of choices...even within one vegetable! Start with looking at what you purchase from the grocery store – the usual vegetables like salad greens, tomatoes, fresh vegetables and fruit. Then think of things that maybe you would like but rarely see in your local supermarket. For example, a vegetable that your Italian grandparents served but you cannot find a fresh source for. Then

The variety of vegetables and flowers available in seed packets is endless.

2: Evaluate the plants on your wish list.

- Are they good for containers?
- How much space do they need?
- How tall do they get?
- How many plants will grow per foot of space?
- How much sun do they need?

Eliminate any plants on your list that rate as being less than good choices for your specific situation. For instance, a Kentucky Blue Lake green bean vine can reach 8 feet. Although this can be supported on balcony rails laterally, it may not be the best candidate for a container at the edge of a patio. Potatoes are another vegetable to consider carefully. Yes, the tiny new potatoes taste wonderful, but the space each plant takes up versus the amount of potatoes each plant yields is often not space-efficient for you.

At the end of this exercise you should have a reasonable list of potential vegetables to grow.

look at how much you use. A single person might use a head of lettuce per week but only one-third of a large watermelon in that time. Some things store well, which is fine, but the point of growing some of your own vegetables is to be able to harvest and eat them when they are very fresh.

"Can I grow that?"

Once you have an idea of what kinds of veggies you'd like, the reality is that not every vegetable will be happy growing in all conditions. Some need more sun, some are touchy about elbow room, some like to climb. So, look first at your growing conditions and then at what your plants require.

1: Your conditions

- How much sun do I get?
- How large is my growing space?
- Do I have some sort of support structure to use?

Now one last thing: Divide the list into those that are good to grow from seed and those that you intend to purchase as a plant.

Potatoes take up a lot of room.

46

Finding seeds for unusual varieties

Seeds for common vegetables such as lettuce, tomatoes and peppers can be found in many places, from the local nursery to online nurseries. For uncommon varieties of vegetables such as Purple Dragon carrot or Casper eggplant, and heirloom and organic varieties, check out some of these online seed sources and more: Burpee, Baker Creek Heirloom Seed Company, Johnny's Selected Seeds, Renee's Garden Seeds and Seed Savers. Just make sure that whatever variety you choose to grow is suitable for your growing conditions, region and climate.

So many varieties!

When you head to the Internet or pick up a catalogue, or even peruse the seed carousel in the garden store, you will find an overwhelming number of varieties of common herbs or vegetables. For

There are many varieties of basil.

instance, basil comes in green or purple leaf varieties, small globe or large plant habits, and can have white, pink or purple flowers. That is even before leaf size and taste is taken into consideration!

Seeds arrive in just days from ordering, so placing your order early gets you the best selections.

Seed Party!

Each seed packet contains a lot of seeds. Lettuce contains more than tomatoes, but even large seeds like squash have a dozen or more in them. If you want to grow one each of several different varieties of zucchini, you will have a lot of seeds left over. Seeds do store but fresh seed has a much higher germination rate.

A seed party is a group of gardeners who get together at the ordering stage and pool ideas of what you all want. Maybe three people want to grow a really hot pepper and four more prefer a milder cayenne pepper, but you all want to grow a basic bell green pepper. Everyone wants to end up with one plant of each of their selection. As a group you order one pack of cayenne, one hot pepper and one green pepper. When the seeds arrive, you regroup and divide the seeds from the package between you. This is really cost efficient when you all want to grow several varieties of lettuce, tomato and pepper. Add a beverage and snacks to the meetings and general garden chat for a great afternoon or evening in the middle of winter!

Timing is everything

Indoor seed starting is timed so that the seedlings are ready to go into the ground/container when the weather is settled. A major point in the garden calendar is the Average Last Frost Date for spring planting and the Average First Frost Date for fall planting. This is variable, and the actual date of the last frost in spring can be up to two weeks from that date. In general though, the late frosts are light. With this date on the calendar, look at your seed packet (see facing page for how to decipher a seed packet and when to start your seed).

Cool weather crops (i.e., kale, chard, cabbage, salad greens) are generally started 6-8 weeks before the last frost date and warm weather ones (i.e., tomatoes, peppers, summer squash) 3-4 weeks before. Starting extra early does not get you an earlier crop because seeds sown indoors too early end up being straggly and unhealthy unless they are given lots of light. Competition for window and light space is a common issue when you get lots of little seedlings all jostling for sunlight. It helps tremendously if you delay the warm weather seedlings until the cool ones are almost ready to move outside.

These tomato seedlings are ready to be transplanted into containers.

Deciphering a Seed Packet

Basic growing information is on the back of most seed packets. Look for:

Depth to sow the seed – Large seeds are planted deeper than shallow ones.

Days to emerge – This varies from 5-15 days for most seedlings.

Days to maturity – This is usually after the seedlings have been put outdoors and is an approximate number. Weather is a big factor in whether your harvest will be on time!

Spacing – This tells how far apart you should space your plants in the garden. Usually row spacing, too.

Size – Vining plants grow anywhere from 3-8 feet, and this is usually noted so that you can be ready with the right support.

Container – For smaller varieties of traditionally large plants, this may give an indication that they are appropriate for containers.

Start indoors – Tells how long before your last frost date you should start the seeds indoors. Warm weather plants are usually 4-6 weeks before the last frost.

Sow outdoors – Tells when to sow the seed outdoors. Some seeds like to have the soil warm before they will germinate, so soil temperatures are given.

Not all these items will be on every pack, but the basics for being successful with that specific vegetable will be noted.

Starting Seeds Indoors

Pellets and mixes. Seed starting kits are commonly purchased with dry, fibrous pellets that expand when wet. These are easy to ship and convenient for the consumer. Follow the guidelines to hydrate the pellets before you sow seed in them. Sow one seed per pellet.

Seed starting mixes are also available and are lighter than general growing mixes. Moisten the mix prior to filling growing cells or containers and put one seed per cell or several in a larger container. Close the lid on the container (if it has one) or place some plastic wrap over the top to keep the moisture in until the seeds germinate.

Germination. Germination takes 5-10 days in a warm home, and the little seedlings will need bright light almost immediately – so be ready! Remove the covering from the seedlings as soon as they have germinated so that you don't get fungal issues.

The first leaves that a seedling produces will be a simple set of basic leaves. (Tomatoes, peppers, basil and lettuce all look about the same.) The second set of leaves are the true leaves, and the differences between varieties is apparent.

Transplanting. When a seedling has two sets of real leaves it can be transplanted into a larger container if you have one. Seedlings should be transplanted to a larger pot before the roots all get tangled together. The growing medium for the larger containers can be the same as the seedling mix

Seed pellets – compressed (left) and expanded (right).

Container with growing cells. These seedlings have their basic leaves.

but a little light fertilizer is added. Alternately, the move can be to a container with a regular potting mix that includes fertilizer. Transplant the seedlings one final time into their permanent garden space when the ground is warm enough for them to grow well.

Extending the season. Frosts both at the start and end of the normal growing season kill young plants unless they are protected. Cover the raised bed or container with a light cloth to prevent the frost from touching the plants and keep them alive. Covering with more sturdy clear plastic panels also keeps the frost away and creates a small cold frame where vegetables can be started much earlier outside than normal. It also allows the cool weather lettuce to survive into winter.

Fertilization

We expect a lot from our vegetable plants, and just as we need good food, the plants do too. Most of the nutrients are taken up from the soil or potting medium, but the continued production that is expected from them requires some extra boosting from fertilizers.

The first rule of fertilization is Read the Label! Too much fertilizer or the wrong dilution can kill the plant rather than help it. Strengths for seedlings and grown plants will be different and each product will have different application rates.

Fertilizers come in a various forms: liquids that can be sprayed or mixed through a hose-end container, or granular, which is meant to be spread around the plants. Always read the instructions for application and dilution before you start.

Organic or chemical? Fertilizers can be organic or chemical. The main source of nitrogen in chemical fertilizers commonly comes from urea, which is taken up by the roots or through the leaves and creates a very green plant, just as it does in the lawn. These are fine for your flowers if you want rapid growth but not so good for your vegetables. As against the lawn, which grows rapidly and is then mowed, the over-fertilized vegetables spend a lot of time putting out new leaves but very few flowers and fruit. The rapid growth also creates large, tasteless green vegetables…and really, do you want healthy vegetables to eat or chemicals?

Natural or organic sources range from manures to compost-based blends plus liquid fertilizers, and frequently include plant elements too. Organic fertilizers generally have much lower NPK (nitrogen, phosphorus and potassium) numbers than chemical fertilizers; the front of the package will show you the numbers.

What is NPK?

When you look at any bag or bottle of fertilizer you will see three numbers on the front, although one or more might be zero. These refer to the basic or macronutrients that a plant needs: N for Nitrogen content; P for phosphorus and K for potassium. A good way to remember what these nutrients do is to think "Up, Down, All Around": nitrogen (up) is good for upward growth and vegetation; phosphorus (down) is good for root and overall growth and development; and potassium (all around) is good for cell development, photosynthesis and all around health.

Seeing the NPK number on the front of a fertilizer gives you an idea of major nutrients in that particular product, but looking at the ingredients indicates what else is in there. It is important to know what the other ingredients do because roses and African violets need different fertilizers than tomatoes and summer squash.

What about Compost?

Mixed or single source? In the early days of organic growing, fertilizer came from bloodmeal (dried animal blood) for nitrogen and bonemeal (ground animal bones) for phosphorus. Feather meal (ground, processed poultry feathers) could also be found. These are single source fertilizers and should contain nothing else. Mixed fertilizers are a blend of a variety of sources to give a range of macro and micronutrients as well as the main NPK numbers.

Compost is derived from decomposed organic garden material. Commercial sources can use farm-derived bulk material such as alfalfa or mushroom compost. But you can make your own compost, using kitchen scraps and garden waste. Compost contains a wide range of nutrients that were held in the original material, so it provides a great addition to the garden.

Manure or composted manure. This is derived from animal waste and includes well-decomposed manure from horse farms, chicken farms or earthworms. The nutrients in the manure are dependent on what the animal took in, but they are generally a good source for both major and secondary nutrients. Take care that the manure is well decomposed so that there are no residual pathogens and that they do not burn your plants. This is particularly important if you are using a local horse farm for your manure. Do not use the waste from cats or dogs, as the pathogens in these materials are harmful to humans.

Compost tea/manure tea. This is a liquid form of compost and is made in a similar fashion to any other tea. The liquid contains almost all the original nutrients but in a more dilute form. Compost tea can be used as 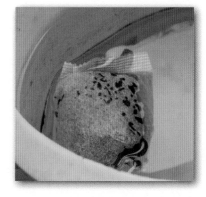 a foliar stimulant too if it is sprayed directly onto the leaves so that the nutrients are absorbed there rather than through the root system. New no-mess tea bags are now available that you set to steep in a bucket of water and use the next day. Remove the tea bag and return it to the compost pile. (For more about the various types of non-chemical fertilizers and what they do, see Appendix page 167.)

How and When to Fertilize

Your vegetable plants all require lots of great nutrients to produce well and consistently (this is particularly important to remember when you are growing in a container). The first time to think about fertilizer is when you prepare the raised bed or container. A nice dose of compost to the bed, or manure to the potting mix, will give the plants a good start. Seeds that are rinsed in compost tea get the immediate benefit of the nutrients as they start to grow.

Tip: For small seeds such as lettuce or pepper, sow the seeds as normal and give a light water of compost tea before you leave them to germinate.

For a second-year raised bed, it is best to add a good application of compost or manure to the bed in fall and again in spring to give the fertility a boost. For containers, empty the whole thing and refill with new mix, as the vegetables will have pretty much used up all the nutrients last year.

Once the vegetables start growing, they still need some extra nutrients in the growing season, and that can be tailored to your plants, or you can do a general fertilization. Growing plants can be "side dressed" with compost or manures, which means that the shovels of compost are deposited along the side of the plants or row of plants. Or you can broadcast a general granular fertilizer across the bed.

Foliar feeding. This is helpful for individual plants that are ailing. Here, a weak solution of fertilizer is sprayed directly onto the leaves where it can be absorbed quickly. If you do this, you really should shelter the plant for an hour or so, so that the liquid is absorbed and the leaves dry before the sun hits them.

Cover Crops

Until recently, the idea of using cover crops was meant to cover fallow fields on the farm. A fallow field is land that a farmer plows but does not cultivate for one or more seasons to allow the field to become more fertile again. The same theory can be applied to the raised bed or small home garden. Cover crops are fast-growing crops that are sown at the end of the season to grow and produce nutrients for next year. For example, early growing cover crops can be used to nourish the area where warm weather beans are going to planted. Common cover crops include rye, clover and the pea family. The growth is either killed off by winter, in which case the decomposing vines are tilled in at the start of the year – or, for spring cover crops, the whole plants are cut down and tilled into the plot. Cover crops not only provide nutrients to the soil but they minimize erosion of the soil in the bed.

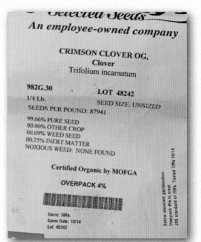

Pollination Notes

No matter if you are growing apples or zucchini, the flowers need to be fully fertilized for successful fruit set. Fruit set is a term indicating whether the flowers on a plant or tree produce fruit or don't produce after pollination. Poor fruit set means little or no fruit on the plant. (And yes, a squash is technically a fruit since it starts out as a flower. So are tomatoes, green beans and peppers.)

For pollination to work, the pollen has to be transferred from one flower to another, and that takes insects and animals. Attracting insects to the garden is as important as creating healthy soil for the plants to grow in. Sometimes the bright flowers of

squash and green beans are sufficient to attract the pollinators, but far more will arrive if you create a vegetable patch that has some flowers in it too. Calendulas, marigolds and basil all produce great summer flowers and make your vegetable plot colorful, aesthetic and productive.

A side benefit of lots of color to attract pollinators is that many pollinators also enjoy harvesting those pesky little white flies or aphids that visit the garden and destroy the harvest. But even with pollinators visiting the garden, they can miss your plant. Squash plants need many visitors to fully

fertilize the plant, and at both the start and finish of the season these visitors just may not be around.

Tip: Look for malformed fruit in squash as an indicator that pollination is not successful. In tomatoes, look for shrunken, immature fruit that drops off before growing.

For indoor plants, you might need to help nature along. (Leafy green vegetables such as kales, cabbages and salad greens do not need a pollinator because you are eating the plant leaves before the flower stalk is produced.)

The boys and the girls. Most common plants in the landscape produce flowers with very little help from the gardener. In the edible world it's the fruit we want, not just the flower, so in order to get the fruit, the flower has to be pollinated. However, some plants need to have a mate in order to be fruitful. Tomatoes and peppers are able to manage to produce fruit regardless of how many plants you have; just one plant will produce beautifully for you without a mate. Not so with apples or blueberries (see Chapter Seven for growing fruit in your vegetable garden). Although there are some self-pollinating varieties out there, you really need a second plant that is flowering at the same time. For apples, this pollinator-mate has to be a different variety. For small spaces, just finding the room to grow two trees can be a challenge.

Pollination issues

Pollination outside can be disrupted by many issues that are out of your control. An unusually warm February or March can fool the plant into thinking that spring is here and they put out a flower, only for it to be killed by a late frost when April arrives. Covering small plants or bushes can help protect them, but buds and newly germinated fruit can be destroyed by just one or two degrees of frost. This is particularly an issue if you are growing early-blooming fruits such as apricots, which are prone to putting out the flowers a week or two earlier than most fruit trees.

Summer squash produces male and female flowers.

At the other end of the spectrum, excessive heat can also disrupt fruit set. Even tomatoes take a break from flowering when the temperature soars into the mid to upper 90s. Just as you, the gardener, opts for shade in these temperatures, so do the bugs that pollinate the existing flowers.

Pollination indoors.

Indoor growing, whether in a sunny window or greenhouse, is more likely to find pollination issues for obvious reasons – we tend to let the bumblebees and flies stay outdoors! Without these insects, though, you will have to help nature along. A small cotton swab can be used to transfer pollen from one flower to another – for tomatoes, particularly, a small electric toothbrush is suggested. Both of these help shake the pollen from one flower and place it on the receptors in the next flower, just like nature does.

Indoor pollination with a cotton ball.

Moving Things Around: Practical Crop Rotation

Growing the same thing in the same soil for several years is a recipe for disaster. Each group of plants attracts certain nematodes that help it to grow and keep diseases away. Alongside the good guys are some not-so-good nematodes that would like to invade your plants. These remain in the soil from one year to the next and eventually will overtake the good guys and attack the roots of your vegetables.

There is also the issue of nutrients – some plants are hungry for one nutrient while another group takes a different set of nutrients from the soil. Continuously growing the same plant in the same soil will deplete the nutrients that it needs, eventually causing it to fail. So, moving things around each year is a way to keep all these concerns at bay. A standard rotation is every 3 years, but if you have room, a 4- or even 5-year rotation is even better. Check the sidebar at the right for some guidance about your plants' rotation preferences and needs.

The Plant Families

3. Peas and Beans – All the legumes enrich the soil with nitrogen, and for this reason it is great to rotate them about. *Tip:* Follow this group with heavy-feeding tomatoes for good tomato yield.

1. Cabbages and salad greens – Cabbages, cauliflower, kales, lettuce, chards and most leafy greens are in this group. Rotate to avoid nutrient depletion.

2. Potatoes and Tomatoes – These are the most problematic. Soil viruses quickly destroy the plants, so it is particularly important that you rotate these. Include peppers in this group too.

4. Onions and root crops – These are much smaller individual vegetables and can be slotted in among the cabbages row or alongside beans or any of the others, so long as they do not occupy the same place for two years consecutively.

The basic rotation plan. In an 8x4-foot raised bed, rotation is done by dividing the length into three parts and moving the plant families along into the next third the second year. By the time year 4 arrives, the bugs in the first section will, hopefully, have given up.

A mini-rotation. With a smaller 4x4 bed the rotation is not as easy, but a mini-rotation can be achieved by planting a mix of things in the same space during one gardening year. Start by dividing the bed into 4 quarters, each containing 4 squares. In each of the quarters, start the year with some lettuce in one square, some kale in another and maybe a few cabbages or carrots in the other squares. As the temperature heats up in summer, replace the lettuce and kales and plant a tomato. Replant the square again with late season chards. Assuming you move the tomato plant to another quarter next year and continue the succession of planting, you have gone a long way to minimize the problem of rotation.

Like me, like me not. Crop rotation and replanting every few weeks is great, but small garden areas will still have crops from different families close to each other. This sometimes causes "like me, like me not" problems in the plant world. Just as black walnuts are known to send out toxins to stop almost anything growing near them, so do some vegetables, and although they are not as virulent as black walnut, they can still mess up your planting scheme. There are numerous resources around that talk about companion planting, which includes who grows well with what and who does not; it is worth taking the time to check before you plan the garden.

Some common garden companions:

- Peas and beans get along with salad greens and cabbages (but are not good with onions).
- Onions grow well with carrots and the cabbage group (but not beans).
- Lettuce and cabbages, etc., do well with beans (but not tomatoes). ▦

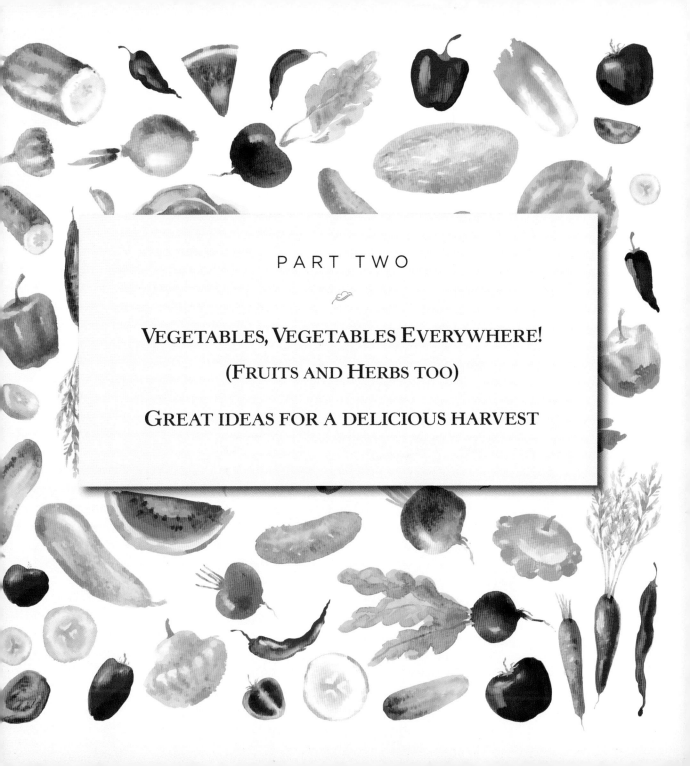

PART TWO

VEGETABLES, VEGETABLES EVERYWHERE!

(FRUITS AND HERBS TOO)

GREAT IDEAS FOR A DELICIOUS HARVEST

FOUR

Growing Veggies Outdoors in the Garden

Now let's see what grows best for your own situation and available space. This chapter is filled with suggestions for how to maximize what you've got, while keeping things manageable – and most of all, enjoyable. We'll look at planting strategies (and plant choices) for creating a bountiful harvest. *Note:* For more detailed growing and plant selection information, see Part Three: The Veggie Garden Growing Year: Plant by Plant, Season by Season.

The Small-Space Garden

Small properties or a small area used for growing vegetables can be very productive if you've planned carefully. In Chapter One, I described the Square Foot Gardening method, which uses just one square foot to grow a tomato or cabbage or multiple carrots or scallions. Replanting the same square several times in the growing year optimizes the use of the space, maximizes the production and keeps weeds away as well! Let's say you want to plant a 4x4-foot raised bed garden using this method – you'll have 16 individual "square-foot" squares to work with. You can fill each square with a single plant or with seeds…or you can take a side of 4 consecutive squares and have a "row" crop such as beans or peas.

A simple plan. I like to draw the bed on paper and lightly pencil in the 1-foot squares. My plans generally have about 2 inches for each square; and then I make three more copies, one for each main growing season. Decide what you are going to grow based on your lists from the previous chapter.

Start your garden in spring or early summer by filling the raised bed with about 10 cubic feet of good mix (see page 32). The beds can also be started in mid-summer or even fall, but the amount of produce you can grow diminishes as the weeks go by.

Spring and early summer: planting tips for a continuous harvest

The stars of the early vegetable garden are the kales, chards, and salad greens like lettuce and mesclun. These leafy green vegetables enjoy cool weather and grow well even in dull, cloudy weather. For a maximum harvest, start some of the vegetables indoors 8-10 weeks before the last frost date. These will be seedlings by early spring and can be planted in the garden space allocated – about 2 or 3 per square.

At the same time as I am planting out the seedlings, I like to sprinkle a few extra seeds in the area so that while I am harvesting the kale (for example) from the mature seedlings, the new seeds are germinating and growing. These new seedlings mature and are harvested after the first batch is finished, giving me a continuous harvest for many weeks in spring.

Harvesting kale and chard. Kale and chard are harvested by trimming the leaves rather than taking the whole plant. The stalk will continue to produce new leaves, which quickly grow to harvestable size, and they will be productive until the second batch of seeds is up and producing for you. When the older plants are finished, carefully cut each stem to the ground, rather than digging or pulling it out. That is because the younger plants have roots that are close to, or interwoven with, the roots of the older plants; these tender young roots would be disturbed if you pulled out the plant complete with all its roots.

Lettuce and mesclun can be started indoors at the same time as kale and chard. Again, for a long, continuous harvest, sow some new seeds as you plant the lettuce seedlings.

Harvesting lettuces. Lettuce comes in both head and loose-leaf forms, and you harvest each in a different way. Head lettuce is left until the head is fully formed, at which time you cut the whole plant for harvest. Leaf lettuce and mescluns are harvested on a "cut and come again" basis and will continue to produce all through the spring.

Regional tips. In colder areas, a cold-tolerant lettuce is a good choice for the start of the season; as spring turns to summer you can transition to a variety that enjoys some heat. In the warmer South and elsewhere, start the season with standard spring lettuce varieties, and then for the main crop, transition into those that tolerate warm weather. In regions where winters are cool (not cold), with very little frost, you can plant an extra-early winter crop of cold-tolerant lettuce (see page 149 for cold-tolerant varieties). If a frost is expected, you should cover the lettuce with a light cloth.

6 Nutritious Leafy Green Vegetables for Spring

Kale – Comes in many sizes and varies from blue to dark green.

Mesclun – Lots of colorful leaves to add to your salad.

Loose leaf lettuce – These do not form the usual lettuce head and can be harvested as soon as the leaves are about 4 inches long.

Spinach – Deep green and fast growing, spinach can be harvested as young leaves for salads. Mature leaves can be stir-fried with a little garlic for a great side dish or added to soups or vegetable sautés.

Chard – Colorful red, fuchsia and yellow-gold stalks with bright green leaves. Leaves and stalks are edible both raw and cooked and make a colorful addition to many dishes. When cooking mature leaves, add the stems first, then add the leaves (the thick stems take a little longer to cook).

Microgreens – Tiny, young vegetable greens that are smaller than baby greens but harvested later than sprouts. They range in size from 1-3 inches, including the stem and leaves. Plants used as micro-greens can include red cabbage, cilantro and radish, providing a variety of leaf flavors from sweet to spicy. Pep up your salad bowl with a handful of microgreens tossed in.

Scallions, shallots and onions. While your lettuce and kales are filling one half of the garden bed, the onion family can be planted in another area. Start scallions, shallots and onions very early in the year, or they can be purchased as young "sets." Plant 10 or 12 of the smaller seedling onions or 4-6 of full-size onions in one square and let them mature into the summer.

Garlic can be grown alongside the onions and is started from individual cloves.

Peas. Peas are another early crop but they take up a little more room in the garden, so for a good crop you will probably want to allocate a full side of the 4x4 raised bed to accommodate them. Pick varieties that grow upward rather than scramble across the ground – and secure the support fence or trellis as soon as you sow the seed (peas are sown directly into the ground outside). A snow pea or other variety with edible pods is fast to mature and will produce for several weeks, but be finished and pulled out in time to plant the beans and peppers. Vines for peas range from just over 2 feet for container varieties to almost 8 feet, but most average 2-4 feet and are easy to support.

The cabbage group. This includes **broccoli, cabbage and cauliflower**. They are cool weather plants but they take longer to mature than the lettuces and kales. Unless you live in a warmer region, these are best started as seedlings rather than planting seeds.

Depending on the variety, cabbages can range from small container sizes, which produce a

1-pound head on average, to standard sizes, which are 3 or 4 pounds each. For two people, a small head yields enough for one or two meals; the larger sizes are great for family meals and preserving.

Cauliflower and broccoli have less variation in size but their time to maturity can range from 50 to almost 80 days! Check the information on the seed packet or catalogue to make sure you are not wasting valuable space waiting for one of these vegetables that take a long time to mature – 30 days is almost a crop of lettuce!

Spring Planting Vegetable Grid

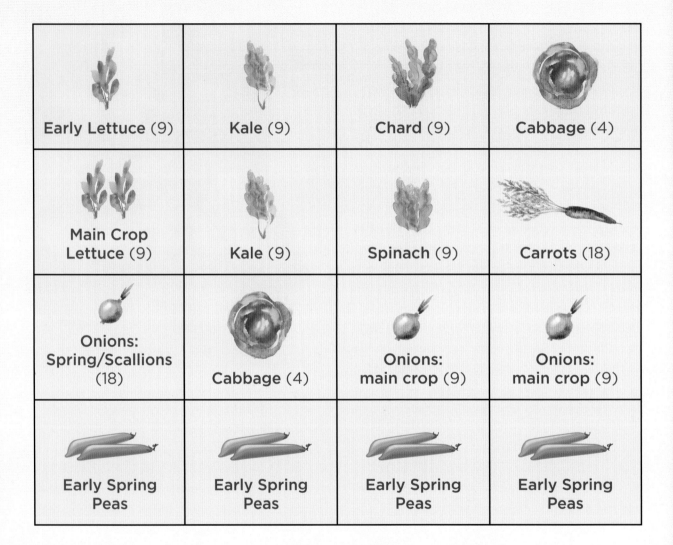

Early Lettuce (9)	Kale (9)	Chard (9)	Cabbage (4)
Main Crop Lettuce (9)	Kale (9)	Spinach (9)	Carrots (18)
Onions: Spring/Scallions (18)	Cabbage (4)	Onions: main crop (9)	Onions: main crop (9)
Early Spring Peas	Early Spring Peas	Early Spring Peas	Early Spring Peas

Transition to summer – the warm weather vegetables

Almost as soon as the spring garden is growing well, summer is upon us and it's time to start thinking about warm weather vegetables – the beans, tomatoes, peppers and summer squash varieties. All these vegetables enjoy, and need, maximum sunlight; best to keep taller plants at the back and shorter ones in front. While spring vegetables do tend to be quite short in height, tomatoes can grow 5 or 6 feet tall and squash vines can ramble for several feet. So be aware of the eventual size of your veggies over the course of the long summer season.

In all but the warmest areas, tomatoes and peppers need to have been started indoors or purchased as plants. You don't want to wait until past July 4th for the first tomato! Summer squash and beans do not need to be started indoors, but squash particularly needs warm soil, so do not rush any of these into the garden. Beans, on the other hand, will tolerate mild days; I have planted them as much as 2 weeks ahead of the official last frost (if the forecast is good).

5 Summer Vegetables for Small Spaces

Dwarf green beans: Produce normal sized green beans but are very short vines (<3 feet). They work well in containers as well as the garden.

Patio tomatoes: Usually cherry tomatoes or small salad size with about 2-3 foot vines.

Container sweet corn: Reaching about 4 feet high and best planted in groups of 6 or 8 for good pollination. Can be grown in containers.

Patio green or hot peppers: Short, stubby plants with normal size pepper, usually medium to hot on the heat scale.

Summer squash: Has large leaves and does scramble around but can be grown on a trellis. Most people just need one or two of this prolific producer. Look for container varieties that have a more compact growth habit.

Patio eggplant: Compact and smaller fruit – enough for one or two people.

Transitioning the 4x4 spring veggie bed to summer crops

As the weather heats up, the **kales** and **chards** are probably the first to go from the garden – and as both are prolific producers you are probably ready to take a break from them appearing at the dinner table too! Take the whole plant out of the ground and add it to the compost pile (you don't have to worry about roots this time). The **cool season lettuce** is also slowing down and most can be removed. Leave one square for **warm season lettuce** so that you have something to put on the burgers from the grill, but replace the rest with summer vegetables.

The **peas** are probably still producing and will continue until the warm weather really kicks in, but you need to get the **beans** started. The bean seeds can be sown underneath the pea vines; as they germinate, the peas will shield them from excess sun. Once the peas are done producing, you can chop the pea vines down and let the beans grow on the same trellis or fence. Add a little fertilizer to the beans after you remove the pea vines and add fertilizer to all the now-empty squares.

Depending on variety, the **peppers** can be quite small plants but still need one square per plant, and the **tomatoes** definitely need a full square each. Removing the kale, chard and 2 lettuce squares will give you 4 squares to divide into peppers and tomatoes. A little extra room can be found where you have already harvested **scallions** or **carrots** (see below for more about carrots), but try to avoid fitting too many little seedlings into the squares – they grow very quickly into large plants!

The summer squash and melon group. Summer squash and melons are also grown from seed planted directly into the ground. Place these seeds in the squares where the cabbage family are just finishing and being harvested. By the time your squash vine is growing, the cabbages will have been harvested, and by putting the squash vines near the back they can take advantage of the bean trellis, particularly if the trellis is teepee-shaped, where the vines can clamber through the beans and continue onto their own trellis at the back.

Summer Planting Vegetable Grid

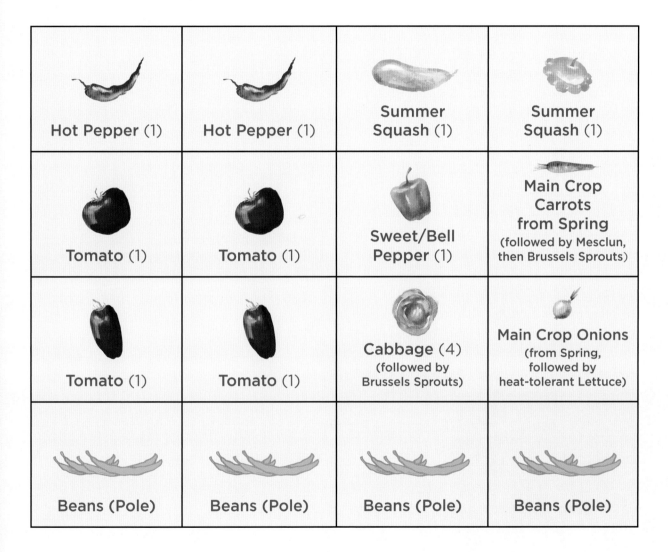

Hot Pepper (1)	Hot Pepper (1)	Summer Squash (1)	Summer Squash (1)
Tomato (1)	Tomato (1)	Sweet/Bell Pepper (1)	Main Crop Carrots from Spring (followed by Mesclun, then Brussels Sprouts)
Tomato (1)	Tomato (1)	Cabbage (4) (followed by Brussels Sprouts)	Main Crop Onions (from Spring, followed by heat-tolerant Lettuce)
Beans (Pole)	Beans (Pole)	Beans (Pole)	Beans (Pole)

Planning the fall garden in mid-summer

Too often the summer garden is thought of as the main garden, and when the fall frost takes those summer vines and crops down, the garden is finished. This does not have to be the case if you plan ahead for the returning cool weather. All those early-season crops from the leafy green group and the cabbage group can be started again! The advantage is that the soil is now warm and the seeds can be planted directly into the ground rather than waiting on your overcrowded windowsill. There are fewer bugs around in fall, and although the rain is still sporadic, it generally becomes more consistent as the summer wanes and temperatures come down. **Focus on fast-maturing varieties.** These would be the **small cabbages**, **baby carrots** and **leafy greens** that mature for a quick harvest. A crop of **snow peas** can start again under the beans to fill out the bed. An alternate location for the peas would be the area where the onions, garlic and scallions were. This allows a few extra weeks for the beans to produce. **Cold-tolerant** lettuce varieties can go into any empty, or soon-to-be-empty, squares.

Plant garlic in the fall.

After the killing frost for the year, the garden will stop producing…except for the cold-weather vegetables such as the **kales** and **Brussels sprouts**, if you grew them. These will continue to flourish after the first frosts. It has been said that the flavor of kales and Brussels sprouts actually sweetens after that first heavy frost. For the rest of the garden, remove all the dead foliage for compost and add a little compost to the beds.

Then order more **garlic**! Yes indeed, this hardy plant can be planted in the fall after the garden has had a good frost. The little cloves produce shoots that stay above ground throughout the winter and then grow vigorously early next spring. Just remember to use a different square for the garlic than last year.

Fall Planting Vegetable Grid

Garlic (9)	Garlic (9)	Garlic (9)	Garlic (9)
Fall Lettuce (9)	Kale (9)	Chard (9)	Brussels Sprouts (4)
Fall Lettuce (9)	Fall Carrots (18)	Brussels Sprouts (4)	Spinach (9)
Snow/Snap Peas	Snow/Snap Peas	Snow/Snap Peas	Snow/Snap Peas

4 Tips for a Successful Small Garden

- Do not over-plant and crowd the plants – this leads to poor air circulation and struggling plants.
- Do not replant the same thing in the same spot – move things to another square.
- Read the label and put plants that will be taller behind shorter ones.
- Water and fertilize regularly – we expect a lot from the garden, so give it some help along the way.

The winter garden

A small 4x4 garden bed can produce a huge amount of produce during the growing year, but if you cover the bed in fall, some of those vegetables will stay ready for harvest into the middle of winter. Winter sun can keep the top layer from freezing, and snow insulates the ground and raised bed too. You can keep the crops from dying by covering the bed with hay and using an old window or rigid plastic sheet laid over the frame of the raised bed (these come in 2x8-foot sheets from the hardware store). By covering the bed you have, in effect, made a little cold frame, which you can use to start those cold weather vegetables earlier next year – as well as harvest lettuce in January!

4 Plants for a Winter Cold Frame

Kale: Pick cold-hardy Russian varieties.

Spinach: Thrives in cool temperature and tolerate some frost.

Carrots: These should be fully grown and mature but can be kept in the ground until you need them – think of it as an outdoor refrigerator.

Cold-tolerant lettuce: See page 149 for some cold-tolerant varieties. The plant will go dormant in the middle of winter but start growing again very early in the year.

Expanding the garden bed

Do you have room for a larger garden? The examples so far have been for a small, 4x4-foot garden bed. The same planning can be used for an 8x4-foot bed. Longer crops like Brussels sprouts would then become an option for you, as well as giving more room for the peas and beans. For a longer harvest, divide the bed into two parts lengthwise, giving yourself 2x4-foot squares along the length. Plant one 4-foot length with the earliest peas, then the second half of the row with main crop peas. As spring moves to summer, remove the early peas to start the early beans, followed by the main crop beans in the second half after the main crop of peas finishes. Reverse this again in fall by planting first one half of the row with peas, then the second half.

Succession planting of peas and beans.

Using the Vertical Plane in the Small Garden Space

Small gardens very quickly become filled with growing vegetables. The once-small squash plants that you purchased in little 4-inch pots are now 2 feet high with enormous leaves and spreading past their designated one-foot square.

Cages and trellises

Tomatoes and sometimes peppers are typically supported with cages or trellises, as they can sprawl over the ground, but squash and melons can also be supported in the vertical plane. Usually a sloping metal or plastic trellis is better for squash, as the fruit can be large and heavy in some varieties. When the supporting trellis is placed at the outside edge of the garden, it keeps all the foliage and young fruit off the ground where other plants are growing.

Peas and beans are another group of plants best grown in the vertical plane. These are more flexible and have lighter fruit than squash, so a frame laced with string will be sufficient for the branches to clamber up.

4 vegetables that like to be vertical

Beans: Bush beans have vines just a few feet long; pole beans can range from 8-10 feet.

Peas: Most peas are short vines rarely reaching over 4 feet.

Melons: Very sprawling but can be corralled onto a fence or support.

Summer squash: Vines extend several feet but are easy to support on a short trellis.

Some tomatoes need a strong support, while other patio varieties are happy with a light support or a bucket to trail down. The "upside down" tomatoes are a great example of tomatoes growing downward rather than upward, but I have found that this works better with a small tomato variety rather than a larger one.

Support structures are best placed in the garden before or at the same time as you plant. Seedlings and germinating seeds all have small roots that are easily disrupted and broken, but more mature plants have roots that are spreading farther from the stalk; breaking these roots puts undue stress on

Raspberries growing vertically.

the plants. It is also a lot easier to get a plant to grow up an existing trellis or support than it is to corral wild stems and secure them at a later stage. Continue to be vigilant, as these happy plants will grow quickly, and most require encouragement to stay on the trellis as they grow.

Vertical raspberries. The vertical plane can also be used to grow fruit. Raspberries are usually grown as a prickly bush with long stems that are either let to roam free or attached to a fence. Raspberries, though, can also be grown on a stake: place the stake close to the growing crown and attach the stem as they grow upward by encircling the whole clump with a sturdy rope. This idea keeps the stems upright and tidy while still able to produce great fruit. Depending on variety and how big the stems are allowed to grow, your raspberry bush can be trained into a fountain shape as well. See page 115 for more about raspberries.

Three Sisters Planting

Sometimes your vegetables will provide the support for another variety. An example would be the traditional Native American "Three Sisters" garden consisting of **corn**, **beans** and **squash**. The stalks of corn can get to about 5 feet in height, providing the support for the green beans. The beans, in turn, fix nitrogen into the ground to help nourish the corn. The large leaves of the squash grow around the base of the plants and act as a living mulch that provides shade for the roots and helps to conserve water. So not only does this traditional way of growing allow you to grow three different vegetables in the same space as one, but by doing so all the plants mutually benefit from each other.

Espalier techniques

Espalier is a centuries-old method of training a plant or tree to grow against a wall or fence. Elaborate designs made espaliered trees into an art form as well as creating a method of growing fruit. Typically, the fruit in winter was grown in a walled garden that was protected (in northern Europe, this made it possible to grow fruit such as peaches). Espaliers were also found along footpaths and as part of arbor tunnels. These features tended to be in gardens of the wealthy who had troops of gardeners to train the trees over decades of growth.

Espalier though does not have to be just for large gardens – it can be used in small gardens too! Apples, peaches and most fruit trees can be espaliered, making it possible to grow fruit in a small garden. Many fruit trees require another tree to be close by for pollination, and even with dwarf trees this takes up room in the garden. Small trees that are grown at the edge of the garden and espaliered along a fence take only minimal garden space. With careful trimming, you can easily find room for not only 2 apple trees, but maybe another fruit tree too. See page 112 for more about fruit trees.

Like the support for annual vegetables, the espalier form should be established before the tree is too big.

Starting an Espalier

- The "header" of the sapling is cut off so that side limbs are encouraged to grow.
- On the wall or fence attach nails to support the growing tree.
- Wrap wire around the nails and make several horizontal lines along the wall.
- As the tree grows upward and reaches a line, attach it to the wire.
- Trim any forward or backward-growing stems, as well as any stems that grow between the established lines.

5 Themed Gardens for Small Spaces

Much of this book talks about using the Square Foot way of growing vegetables. But there is nothing to stop you veering from that design, particularly after your first season of growing, when you have a feel for what the plants do. The gardens can be tailored to your specific culinary tastes or they can be designed just for fun. Always keep in mind that the plants will still grow and need the same cultural conditions even though they are not in predefined squares.

1. A Pizza Wheel Garden – Oregano and tomato are the base for most pizzas and both grow well in small gardens, as do basil and other herbs; add a side salad and your meal is complete. To make a Pizza Wheel Garden:

- Using a 2-foot piece of string, position one end in the center of the bed and run the other end around inside the square, making a furrow that defines the circle for the pizza.
- Still using the 2-foot piece of string, mark the circle at 8 even points to define the individual pieces of pizza.
- Plant the herbs along the 8 cutting lines of the pizza and fill the segments with lettuce, tomato and pepper plants. *Tip:* Paste tomatoes are better for making the sauce but any variety will work fine.

2. A Happy Face Garden – This is perfect for small children. Over the summer the face will provide tiny tomatoes and lettuce for your child to enjoy. Like the Pizza Wheel Garden, the Happy Face Garden is based on a 2-foot diameter circle.

- The hair: Plant mesclun, salad or other leafy green vegetables around the top of the circle for the hair.
- The smile: Plant red lettuce or red basil for the smile.
- The eyes: Plant 2 patio tomatoes for the eyes.

3. An Italian Garden – The regional gardens are based more on content than design and vary according to what you enjoy eating. The Italian Garden will focus on herbs such as oregano and basil, as well as a wide variety of greens, tomatoes, squashes and peppers.

4. A Mexican Garden – Mexican food is more based on corn, hot peppers and beans, so a variety of shelling beans will be a good start for this garden. Since sweet corn and beans both take up a good amount of space, you might want to plant the chili pepper in a separate container. Include greens and herbs like basil and cilantro to round out the enjoyment of your Mexican Garden.

5. A French Culinary Garden – French cookery traditionally uses herbs such as French tarragon, sage, lavender, thyme and bay leaves – no chili peppers! Pencil-thin French beans work well in the garden along with fresh tomatoes and garlic. *Tip:* Of course you won't be growing a large bay laurel tree in your small raised bed, but you can plant one in a separate container, keep it trimmed to manageable size and reap a bounty of bay leaves for your French cooking. ▪

Containers: the Answer for Patios, Porches, Balconies and Sunny Windowsills

Not everyone is able to grow plants directly in the ground, but that shouldn't stop a determined vegetable gardener! Containers and windowsills make it possible for even those with little or no outside space to still grow some great veggies. If you live in an apartment or condo, you should be able to find room for at least a container or two of vegetables or herbs. In a townhouse environment, for example, where you want to sit outside with a book in the morning and not be on view, a few strategically placed container plants can be the start of a very effective, edible privacy fence (more about privacy planting below).

With container gardening, the key is to optimize the space you have without it being too cluttered.

Containers on tables, railings and vertical stacking all help make the most of limited space.

A Gardener's Seaside Solutions

Betty Bentsen lives on an Atlantic Ocean inlet on the Jersey coastline. Her raised home has wonderful views but very little land to grow vegetables in, so she uses the space on the deck (which leads directly to the boat launch), and a few very small in-ground areas to grow. Gardening in containers, Betty is able to grow a variety of vegetables to enjoy all summer. The coastal winds make it essential to protect the growing vegetables for much longer than inland growers have to, and this year her growing year has been delayed because a duck decided to nest in one of her containers.

Cool coastal winds mean that containers have to be covered for longer than most plants would.

A variety of vegetables in containers line the deck.

The front entrance area

Do you have a small porch area by your front door? If it has good sun exposure, it's a good place to grow a few vegetables. A mixed container that blends some colorful flowers alongside some vegetables makes for a welcoming sight, as well as being productive.

For a large container in full sun, an aesthetic arrangement will have something tall for the focal point, something to fill the surface area and something draping over the side. A focal point could be a **dill** or **fennel** in the center, or even a **tomato** plant. For the filler plants, try **spring lettuce**, followed by **summer basils**; these can be harvested frequently to keep them producing. Basils come in a variety of colors and sizes, including purple ones and small leaf ones that are small enough for a window box. Pick several different basils to get tasty as well as colorful leaves for your recipes. For plants that drape over the side, think about small **squash**, **strawberries** or **patio tomatoes**. Add in a flower or two, like calendula or marigold, and you will have a great summer display to greet your guests.

A patio container garden

If you have a small sunny patio area in the back where you can garden, then the opportunities are slightly better. Containers that might be too large for entrance areas can be placed on patios. Here, aesthetics are still important but the "curb appeal" can be a little more relaxed. Containers come in a

variety of different sizes and materials (see page 161), with lots to choose from. Pottery and classic clay look slightly more formal than cloth bags or plastic, so start with a style that you feel comfortable with in your environment. If the container is about 12 inches in diameter, then it is large enough for a **tomato** or **pepper** plant in the summer. A slightly larger 18-inch container is big enough to grow some **green beans** or **spring peas,** too.

With a patio, you can have room for groups of containers, with a different herb or vegetable in each one. Place one large container in the back and several smaller ones in the front. I often keep a bowl of mixed herbs or salad greens on the patio table so that guests can snip leaves onto their burgers or salads.

85

Annual Herbs for Containers

Basil: Lots of different colors, leaf size and flowers.

Marjoram: Similar to oregano but milder – popular in European recipes.

Cilantro: Replant every few weeks to keep a good supply all summer.

Parsley: A biennial that you need to buy each year.

Mexican tarragon: The annual alternative to true French tarragon. Has a pretty yellow flower.

Dill: Great for a tall item in container designs.

For more about herbs and how to grow them, see Chapter Six.

Grow bags. These are the smallest and least formal containers but they will sit conveniently near a corner of the patio. See page 166 for more about them. The bags can be purchased ready-made and include holes in the bottom for drainage and an X in the top to cut for planting the vegetable. But you can make your own with a bag of regular container mix. Although the bags are generally meant to grow just one item, you can increase the produce with some little adjustment. For a container-mix bag, do a smiley: 2 X's in the top of the bag and a long smile-shaped slit underneath the X's. Use the smile for **early lettuce,** followed by planting 2 **tomatoes** or one tomato and one **pepper** in the X spots. Not a fan of salad? Use one X for a tomato and one for a squash plant. Water the bag regularly and fertilize every few weeks to keep the plants productive.

Patios are a great place to sit with a coffee or cocktail with friends, as well as somewhere to put the barbecue and do messy chores. When you add multiple containers to this mix of uses, your patio could become cluttered and even dangerous, so make sure that you have a pathway clearly established. If the "growing bug" takes hold and you increase the number of containers each season and each year to grow just one more thing…one day you might not be able to turn around!

Look what's growing in a bag of container mix!

Small individual containers. For vegetables, the smallest size should be approximately equivalent to one square foot of growing space. Using the guide in Chapter Two, you will be able to grow one **eggplant**, one **pepper** or several **lettuce** plants in each of the containers. Cluster these together in one area and you have a full veggie garden in containers and close by. Small containers also work well for herbs, which are great for summer cooking. Just as in the garden bed, you can rotate the plants in your containers by the season: **lettuce** and **kale** in the early spring, replaced with **squash** and **eggplant** for summer, etc. Be sure to change the soil between plantings to maximize the nutrients available to the summer plants.

Plants for larger containers. A larger container can, of course, grow more things at the same time, but it is also heavy to move, so make sure that it is in the right place before you start. Along with the

selections given for the smaller containers, you can now try some of the more traditional upright or row crops such as **beans** and **peas**. Some varieties are specially developed for container growing, so use these if you see them.

Container peas grow on vines that are only 2 or 3 feet long, which are easily supported with a short trellis (regular peas can have vines as long as 7 feet), and which produce well when grown in containers in full sun. A certain amount of succession planting can also be achieved with larger containers: plant a few seeds each week and get a much longer harvest. This works with many plants like **lettuce**, **mesclun**, **peas**, **beans** and **carrots**.

Succession Planting Tips for Large Containers

With larger seeds such as peas, start one set of peas in an early container and a few weeks later start some more in a separate container. As the production on the first container wanes, take it out and replace with bean seeds. The second pea container will still be producing while your early beans are growing. Whether or not the peas will continue to grow and mature until the beans start producing depends very much on the weather – too hot too soon is great for beans, but the peas will wilt quickly. However, a long mild spring will keep the peas growing a few weeks longer and overlap with the first bean harvest. Replace the peas in the second container with beans when the peas are finished. A third container starts with leafy spring greens and moves onto summer squash and/or eggplant. Add one more container for the tomato and peppers to grow and you have a complete garden in a very modest space.

One of the biggest advantages of container growing is the mobility factor. All but the largest containers can be moved if needed, which is a boon for early and late season growing.

Getting an early start on the growing season. I like to start a medium-size container – around 16-18 inches across – with seeds of **peas** or **beans**, which will grow in a sunny window inside until the snow melts and early spring arrives. They are then put onto the deck to enjoy mild spring days and brought back indoors on cold frosty nights. I also start a few tomatoes indoors a week or two early. These are transplanted into a container and kept indoors until the warm days of late spring arrive. By growing **tomatoes** in containers indoors for a few weeks, it gets me weeks ahead of Mother Nature and neighbors who are waiting for the ground to warm up. Put the container on a support with wheels so that you can take it outside on mild days and

bring it back in for cold nights as needed. This maneuver works well for early growing where the vines and plants are quite small and manage-able, but is slightly trickier at the end of the season when the plants are much larger and producing well. For the occasional cold spell, I keep a cloth or towel handy and wrap that around the container – but when sustained cold weather arrives, bring the whole container inside and you'll get a few more weeks of produce. Eventually, the day length shortens so much that plants just cannot get enough daylight even in a sunny window. Putting extra lights over the plants helps, particularly for lettuce and small plants, but is rather impractical for mature beans and squash plants.

These flowering peas are getting ready to climb up the trellis.

Balcony growing

Assuming that your balcony gets some sunlight, you will be in good shape for growing a nice variety of vegetables. With all the types of containers available now (traditional, vertical, hanging – even straddling the railing), you should be able to plan a bountiful balcony garden.

If you are starting your veggies from seed, you'll want to find somewhere to start them indoors. I found that an indoor laundry area, under a bed (use a plastic garbage bag under the trays) or on top of the refrigerator are all good options. Just keep an eye on the seed tray and make sure that you take it out of the low light area promptly, because although germinating seeds do not really need sunlight, the minute the seedlings pop up they do.

If you share your apartment with kitties like I did, take extra care that they do not dislodge or tip the container over.

Once the seedlings have germinated, they need to be placed in a warm, sunny location. Ideally, this will be a windowsill or on a table in front of the balcony door. Early vegetables such as kale or spinach can manage in a cool room, but **tomatoes** and **peppers** really need a warm area to grow successfully. On mild days I like to move the seedlings outside the door so that they get used to being in a breeze and full sun. This is called "hardening off."

While you wait for the weather to settle, get your containers for the vegetables filled with good organic potting mix. Cool weather vegetables such as salad greens and chards can be put outside permanently as soon as the worst of winter has moved on. Balconies are often sheltered from wind, and if you put the container close to the wall they will be quite happy even if the night temperatures gets to the mid- to lower 30s. Again, I keep an old towel handy to cover a container just in case a frost is forecast. These leafy early vegetables can also be grown in containers that sit on or over the deck railings, which leaves a little more room for you to move around. *Tip:* When thinking about salad greens for your balcony, here are a few good ones: **sprouts**, **baby chard** and **radicchio**.

These space-saving containers are made to fit over balcony railings and fences, like this chain-link. They are designed to also sit securely on a flat surface.

Vertical stacking. Balconies, like decks, can become cluttered with containers very quickly, so the new vertical stacking containers are great to optimize your space. Check that the containers in the upright system are deep enough for larger vegetables such as tomatoes, but most will easily accommodate small-rooted vegetables like **salad greens, cabbages, onions, peppers, herbs** and even **strawberries.** With the equivalent of 3 containers stacked on top of each other, you can grow a decent selection of great tasting vegetables.

A 3-container planting plan for small balconies. An example of using 3 containers on a small balcony, either stacked or separate, would be to start the first container with **kales, chards** and **spinach.** These can all take a light frost and are very happy with cool spring weather. About two weeks later, plant a second container with **salad** and **mesclun greens.** These are not quite as frost tolerant as the kales but they do enjoy spring sunshine and tolerate cloudy days, too.

The third container is for the summer vegetables; it cannot be planted until the late spring or even early summer heat arrives. Plant one or two **peppers** in this container. By now, the kale container is probably done producing and your household may be tired of eating leafy greens, even if they are good for them! Transition this container to become the **tomato** container. The salad greens are also over by late spring and you have a choice for what you plant here for the summer. If the container can be placed in a location that does not

This creative vertical system gives you 5 containers of various sizes.

91

get hot afternoon sun, you can replant this salad container with **heat tolerant lettuce**.

For full-sun containers that bake in the summer, try a patio-sized **eggplant** or **zucchini**, which love the heat. As the summer cools into fall temperatures, replant your containers with spring greens and lettuces. With just a little protection on nights where there is a chance of a light frost, these cool season containers will last well into fall before they are finally felled by winter and laid dormant until another spring.

If there is room for a fourth container, you can grow **spring peas** followed by **green beans**. These need larger containers than the kales and peppers, but they do double duty by providing some privacy screening for you. Garden troughs that are 12 inches deep by 2-3 feet long are perfect for these traditional row crops. *Tip:* Place a trellis behind the containers before the peas and beans get very big and enjoy harvesting the peas without bending down.

More Container Herbs

Bay laurel
Thyme
Mint
Summer savory
Fennel

For more about herbs and how to grow them, see Chapter Six.

Planting for privacy: a living fence

Patios, balconies and decks give us much more than just a place for our vegetable container garden; this is where we gather with friends or just enjoy being alone. Privacy can be a real issue, especially in a densely built townhouse or condo development. If there isn't a fence or barrier between the next units and yours, there might be rules against adding one. But there is nothing to prevent you from making a living, temporary fence. A living fence of vining, edible plants is very doable and attractive. The first step is to decide which vining plants you want to grow and if you want them to grow up from the ground or down from a hanging basket.

A pole bean "fence": The most vigorous and dense vines are provided by **pole beans**, which come with attractive flowers as well as colorful and healthy beans. Their common flower colors are red, white

and purple, with green, yellow or purple for the beans. *What to do:* Line up same-size containers along the side that needs privacy and plant your beans. Support the plants with one trellis that spans all the containers and gives the beans something sturdy to grow on. Within a few weeks you will have your own living fence.

"Three Sisters" in containers. Another option for upright growth is to plant two or three deep-trough containers with sweet corn. Using the Three Sisters planting scheme, you could have corn, beans and squash all growing together, giving you a productive row of containers and a decent amount of privacy as well. For more about Three Sisters planting, see page 78.

Growing Indoors

For those with no outside balcony or patio space, your growing option is indoors, where good outcomes largely depend on available light. But even then there are solutions.

Windowsill gardening. Give your set of herbs or salad greens a bright sunny window and they will grow happily for you. Nothing large, like zucchini or tomatoes, but you can certainly grow **mesclun**, **salad greens** and **herbs** – or even a few **strawberry** plants. Look for new "green window" sets that create plastic shelving – either secured with removable suckers or hung from the ceiling. This type of shelf will support a light window box or individual small containers of plants.

Without a sunny windowsill, you will need to provide extra light. Growing lights are available in most box stores and come in various sizes to fit your containers. Seedlings need to have the light about 2 inches above the soil level, and the light is raised as the seedlings grow. This is fine for **basil** and **lettuce**, but unless the container and light source are quite large, it is not really a great way to get healthy **tomatoes**.

4 Vegetables for Low Light

Lettuce   Mustard

Stir-fry seed blends   Sorrel

Hydroponics. Is there another way to successfully grow vegetables indoors? In a word: hydroponics. Hydroponics has been around for many years, but until recently the growing units were quite large and not particularly attractive. Now, smaller, compact hydroponic units are available. Some come with their own light source, others do not. The idea of hydroponics is that the plant roots are bathed in nutrient-rich liquids that replace the soil environment and make actual soil unnecessary. The liquid is circulated from the bottom well of the unit through a tube, where it is delivered to the plant and then returned to the reservoir at the base. The nutrient solution is changed every few weeks, depending on the size of the plants and the fertilizer type. As with any other type of growing, the plant still needs light, but you won't have the extra expense of soil mixes and you won't have to mess with watering containers except for the biweekly change of the nutrient solution. The key point with hydroponics is to give the plants light and keep the liquid flowing at a steady but not continuous rate. I set a timer to run the pumps for 30 minutes every hour for seedlings – and 1 hour on, 2 hours off for mature plants. Check the instructions in your kit and the recommended rates for the fertilizer used and adjust as needed for your specific plants.

4 Vegetables for Hydroponics

Patio tomato

Leafy greens

Salad greens

Herbs

4 Vegetables for a Vertical Wall

Lettuce and mesclun
Basil and annual herbs
Kales
Spinach

Growing green walls. As most apartments are small and floor space is limited, there are now products on the market for growing up…on walls. Just like the upside-down tomato, green wall systems allow the plants to grow from pockets in a container of growing mix. The individual rectangular or square unit holds the growing mix and stops water dripping down your wall. Most green wall systems recommend starting the plants with the unit flat. Once the plants have a firm hold on the growing medium, hang the unit and wait for your plants to be large enough to harvest. You can grow **tomatoes**, but for average-size "pockets" you are probably better off growing smaller plants. Larger pockets accommodate more roots and therefore larger plants are possible. Just like the other plant ideas, light is the key to getting good produce – so plan to site your green wall where sunlight (or adequate growing lights) will find it. Multiple units can be used to grow more produce, and since the plants are not outside, your **salad greens** can probably be grown all year round. ▨

SIX

Growing Herbs:
12 Great Herbs for Your Favorite Recipes

*H*erbs are so easy to grow in small spaces. The return that you get from having fresh herbs to harvest is well worth the little effort it takes to grow them. Many herbs can successfully be grown from seed. Compared to the "fresh" herbs in the super-market, your homegrown herbs will save you a lot of money too!

As with the vegetable choices, start with herbs that you use in your favorite recipes. Most ethnic recipes use herbs that grow well in that region, so if you like Italian cooking you will want to have some basil and oregano in the garden; for French cooking you will want rosemary, thyme and marjoram. All of these can be grown in containers and none take up much room in the garden. Just make sure that they have good drainage and lots of sun.

Bay Laurel *(Laurus nobilis)*

Bay leaves are used in French recipes, particularly recipes that take a long time to cook. The bay tree is a neat tree that is hardy through zone 7. If you plant it in a protected, sunny area in zone 7, you might find that although the top growth dies back in winter it re-sprouts from the base each year. Where it is hardy, the tree is evergreen and reaches about 20 feet in height. Most gardeners keep the tree much closer to 4 feet and grow bay in a container. You will often see herb gardens with a neatly trimmed bay tree in the center.

Pick the leaves during the growing season as you need them. In areas with cold winters, let the shrub overwinter inside like you overwinter the rosemary. A bright but cool room with just-moist soil will keep the shrub dormant during the short winter days, and by spring you will see bright green new foliage appearing. Bay leaves can be dried but do not do well when frozen.

Basil *(Ocimum basilicum)*

Basil is a standard in culinary gardens and comes in a myriad of colors and sizes. It comes easily from seed so you can try several different varieties. Sow the seed indoors or directly outside after the last frost. Sow a few seeds outside when you plant the seedlings so that you get a summer-long harvest. Basil is like the tomatoes and peppers in that it does like summer temperatures and will not grow in cool 50-degree days. As the plant grows, harvest the growing tips regularly. When you take the growing tip off, the plant responds by putting out two more little stems, and with regular harvesting you will have a beautiful, bushy basil in the garden.

Eventually the basil will want to put up the flower head. At this stage the leaves lose a lot of their flavor, so enjoy the bloom, then harvest from a younger plant.

For Italian cooking, you cannot beat the Genovese-style basils that have large, dark green leaves – which makes it easy to pick and chop them. The basic basil flavor is anise, but lemon is also popular. Leaf color varies from dark green through lighter greens (in lemon basils), and purple ones that vary from green with purple splotches to a dark purple leaf. Mixing these in the garden and in salads makes for colorful combinations. The flowers on the green basils are white, and the purple basils put out an attractive pink flower, making it perfectly suitable for your front garden as well as kitchen garden.

Basil does not tolerate temperatures below 35 degrees, and is why you do not see it in major supermarkets that transport vegetables in cool-temperature trucks. Cut basil can be kept fresh in a glass of water on the counter for a few days. To preserve basil, it is best to add it to another medium like a tomato sauce or stock, which you can freeze successfully. Basil can also be preserved in an herb vinegar (see page 109).

Chives *(Allium schoenoprasum)*

Chives are typically the earliest flower in many gardens. The small clumps work very well in containers where they give the necessary height to attractive arrangements. Although a perennial, it does come easily from seed if you prefer not to buy a plant. A small clump is generally sufficient for most households. In spring, the chives put out a few slightly woody stems that produce the attractive pink flowers (see photo of flowering chives on page 24). After you have enjoyed the flowers, trim the whole plant back to about 2 inches, and wait for the new growth to start. Harvest the individual stems from the base, not the top – chives is not a grass and cutting an inch off the top of the stem leaves the rest of the stalk that, within a day or two, turns brown where you trimmed. Cutting to the base allows new growth to replace it.

There are a few varieties of chives, but for culinary use, the basic chive is the best producer. There are garlic chives (*A. tuberosum*), which is much greener than the regular chive and blooms in fall. The flavor of this variety is slightly more garlic-onion than the spring blooming one; garlic chives produce a white fall flower. When the flowers have faded, you will be left with the attractive seed head. The seeds start out green and then turn to black. The flower head is good for flower arrangement, but should be trimmed before the seeds mature; the very viable seeds can make a mess if they invade the lawn.

Chives can be successfully frozen whole or snipped into half-inch pieces. You can also take a small rooted section of the plant in fall when it is dormant, trim any remaining top growth down, repot and bring indoors. Place the container in a sunny window and it will regrow, giving fresh chives all winter. The pretty pink flowers from spring produce an attractive pink-colored vinegar that has an oniony taste – great for summer salad dressings. See how to make herb vinegars on page 109.

Cilantro/Coriander
(Coriandrum sativum)

Cilantro comes easily from seed. For a full summer of fresh leaves, I sow a small batch every two weeks, starting about the time of the last spring frost. Germination in warm soil is in about a week and the leaves can be harvested as soon as they are large enough for your needs – about a month. After three or four harvests the leaves change from scallop-edged green leaves to a more feathery fern leaf. At this stage, the seed head is being produced. Let the flower complete its cycle and then let the seeds turn from pale green to brown, when you can harvest them as the spice coriander. Do not be tempted to buy a cilantro plant as it does not transplant well, and assuming it survives the transplanting, it puts out the flower head very quickly. Cilantro does not freeze or dry well, so for winter use you can freeze in a sauce – or try sowing a few seeds in a container to grow on the windowsill.

Dill *(Anethum graveolens)*

Dill can be grown easily from seed that is sown around the last frost date, but it will self-seed for following years if you let the seeds form. The spicy leaves are blue-green and feathery, and the plant reaches about 3 feet tall. Toward the end of the summer a flower stalk is formed, which is often used in flower arrangements. The fine leaves are commonly chopped for sauces that accompany fish and egg dishes. Dill doesn't freeze well but can be dried.

Fennel (*Foeniculum vulgare*)

Fennel fronds look remarkably like dill, but have a slightly stronger anise taste and a different flower structure. Both the feathery green growth and the seeds are used in recipes, as well as the thick bulb at the base of the plant. Clearly, to use the bulb you need to harvest the whole plant, so growing one or two fennel plants for the leaf and seed head plus another couple of plants for the bulb gives you a consistent supply of all parts of the plant over the summer. Place fennel at the back of the garden bed or group of containers so that its 4-to-5-foot height does not shade smaller plants. There is also a bronze fennel that makes a striking addition to the garden but does not have the same depth of flavor. If you just want the bulb for your meals, Florence fennel is regarded as having the best flavor.

Mint (*Mentha* spp.)

Whichever mint you decide to grow, it is best to keep it in a container! Mint becomes invasive by sending runners out across lawns and under pathways. It can also produce viable seed, which spreads it even further. Of the many varieties of mint on the market, the two most common for the kitchen are spearmint and peppermint. Spearmint has apple-green, slightly pointed leaves and peppermint has much darker, broader leaves and a red-tinted stem. Flavor varies between the different mints, so rub a leaf between your fingers before you buy the plant. Although seeds are available, most do not produce good strong-flavored mint. This is a case where it is

worth buying the plant, or taking a cutting from a friend's mint patch. Grow mint in full sun in cooler summer areas, and part sun in hotter regions. In all areas keep the containers well watered. Harvest the leaves as soon as they are a few inches high for recipes and sauces. To preserve, harvest before the flower stalk arrives and trim down to about 2 inches from the soil line. Several major harvests per year are possible. The flower does attract pollinators to the garden, but snip off the flowers before they have a chance to produce a mature seed. Mint dries reasonably well and can be frozen. Chopped mint covered with vinegar and processed also works well to preserve the flavor of the herb. Two mints that are commonly used in cocktails and desserts are pineapple and apple mint, which you can generally find. Apple mint, particularly, has a slightly fuzzy leaf.

Oregano and Marjoram
(Oreganum vulgare and O. majorana)

These are culinary twins of the genus *Oreganum*. Oregano (zone 5) is a perennial that is often found in Italian recipes and has a strong, spicy flavor, whereas marjoram (zone 7-9) is a milder flavored, tender perennial that most people grow as an annual; it is more common in French recipes. Both are excellent for containers and small gardens. Plant in full sun to enjoy the leaves in recipes all summer long.

Oregano has many varieties, including a purely ornamental creeping variety. I look for a true Greek oregano sometimes called *O. hirtum* or *O. heracleo-*

ticum. It produces strong upright stems, lots of flavor and easy to harvest leaves. Oregano produces attractive white flowers early in the season which are trimmed back when the flower fades. Harvest the leaves for tomato sauces, pizzas and many other recipes. Oregano is perennial and hardy through zone 5.

Marjoram is also call knotted marjoram – a name that reflects the shape of the flower. It has a much sweeter and milder flavor than the other oreganos. Sow seed indoors for this herb and plant out after the last frost. Start harvesting leaves for recipes when the plants are about 6 inches tall.

Oreganos all dry well and can be frozen.

Parsley *(Petroselinum crispum)*

Parsley is a biennial but is usually treated as an annual. There are two common varieties of parsley: the Italian or flat-leaved parsley and the curly one. Both have the same nutrients and can be used for far more than just a side "decoration" on the plate. There are some small, ultra-curly varieties that also make great borders for flower gardens. Curly parsley grows anywhere from 6 inches to a foot tall; the flat-leaved parsleys are slightly taller. At the end of the first year, the leaves remain green under the snow, and although they are frozen I have still snipped them for winter casseroles. When the snow clears, the herb can be harvested for a little while until the flower stalk is produced. At this stage, the leaves

lose their taste and I put in a new plant. I leave the old plant to put out the flower – which is attractive to butterflies, including the swallowtail – and continue to form the mature seed. These self-sown seeds grow into healthy new parsley plants. Parsley can be dried or frozen to preserve for winter use.

Rosemary *(Rosmarinus officinalis)*

Rosemary is a woody shrub in warm areas and treated as a tender perennial in colder areas. There are many different varieties and cultivars of rosemary. Some are more hardy than others, but zone 7 is about as far north as you can expect them to survive. 'Arp' is considered one of the hardiest varieties. It is possible to bring the plant inside over the winter, where it can still be harvested. Indoors in winter, the plant prefers a cool, bright room with just-moist soil. Too much moisture, particularly in the middle of winter when the day length is shortest, kills the plant. Indoors, rosemary does suffer from scale and aphid-type insects; this makes keeping it

alive over long winters a challenge that most people don't bother with. Buying a new, vibrant plant each spring is worth the expense.

Rosemary likes full sun even in the hot summers and does just as well in containers as it does in the ground. The biggest issue is if you have poor drainage – rosemary does not like wet soil where the roots rot quickly. This is an issue in some southern areas where occasional long, damp winters kill even mature rosemary plants.

Of the varieties of rosemary on the market, your choice should be geared to what you would use it for: smaller, thinner needles are great to chop for sauces and casseroles, and thicker, sturdier needles are better for grilling. One of each type works well for summer cooking. The woody stems on Gorizia make it great for turning into a kabob stick to grill summer veggies, but I do first poke a hole in the tomatoes, squash and other items before I thread them onto the rosemary stick.

Sage *(Salvia officinalis)*

Like several of the other herbs, there are lots of varieties of sage, including the annual bedding *Salvias*. For culinary use there really are only two varieties, the basic garden sage and *S. officinalis* 'Berggarten'. Both are woody perennials, have the same basic flavor and bright blue flowers, but the leaves on 'Berggarten' are much broader than the traditional sage. The woody stems retain a few leaves over winter that can be harvested; however, the fresh leaves of spring taste much better. The leaves can be harvested for much of the summer, starting in early spring before the flowers arrive all the way past the frosts. The production of the flower stalk in spring doesn't interrupt the leaf production and is attractive to pollinators as well. Sage is harvested a few leaves at a time and is strongly scented, so just a few leaves are sufficient for most recipes and one plant is all most households need. Although sage is perennial, it does get very woody, which destroys its neat overall shape, so trim back hard each spring to keep it healthy.

Of the other sages, there are two that have attractive leaves – one has golden leaves (*S. officinalis* 'Aurea'), the other a pink-white leaf (*S. officinalis* 'Tricolor'). Both have some sage flavor but definitely not as strong, so they are not usually used in the kitchen.

Another sage worth noting is the very tender pineapple sage *(S. elegans)*, much larger than the garden sage with light green leaves that are more fruity than savory. The attractive woody plant starts

in spring in a 4-inch container and quickly grows to almost 5 feet tall with an open vase shape that is covered with bright red flowers in late summer. In far northern areas where frost arrives in September, the plants may not have time to flower, but this *Salvia* is still worth growing for its overall attractive shape in the garden. The fruit-flavored leaves are used in cocktails and desserts, but do not dry or freeze well.

Savory – Winter and Summer
(*Satureja montana* and *S. hortensis*)

Summer savory is an easy-to-grow annual; winter savory is a woody perennial. Both look similar to garden thyme with a slightly narrower needle-like

leaf. Winter savory has a more intense pepper-spicy flavor than summer savory. Both enjoy full sun and produce white flowers, with the winter savory flowering in spring, and the summer savory in summer. The overall shape of both plants is small and bushy. In mild winter areas, the winter savory will retain its green leaves right through to spring when the new, brighter green leaves appear. Harvest the sprigs of leaves and strip for use in the kitchen. You can preserve the leaves (on or off the stem) in the freezer. Winter savory is hardy to zone 6.

French Tarragon
(*Artemisia dracunculus*)

True French tarragon is always purchased as a plant, never as seed. The leaves should be glossy and evenly spaced along the stem, which is generally upright, though some are low to the ground. French tarragon is used in classic French cooking and has a licorice flavor. (There *is* a seed tarragon, Russian tarragon; its leaves are wider apart on the stem, not glossy, and the taste is almost nonexistent – which is why it is not recommended for recipes.) The plant comes reliably back each spring in northern climates, but is less successful in areas where winters are mild and prolonged cold (but not necessarily freezing) soil is insufficient to keep the plant dormant. Most winters in zones 4-6b/7 and

higher only have very short periods of below 32 degrees at night. This is generally not sufficient for French tarragon to grow happily. In warmer parts of zone 6 and most of zone 7 I have had better luck keeping the plant in a container. This allows the root zone to benefit from chilly nights that reach down to the low 30s. In milder areas you can get a good tarragon flavor from the Mexican tarragon, actually a pretty, yellow-flowering annual marigold *(Tagetes lucida)* and not a true tarragon.

French tarragon does not produce noticeable flowers. Each summer, the lower leaves tend to turn brown; at this stage, harvest the leaves down to about 4 inches from the base, and within a week or two new growth appears, returning the plant to a pleasing green again. French tarragon can be frozen, but does not really hold the flavor when dried. It is also popular to make tarragon vinegar, which does impart the true flavor to recipes and makes wonderful culinary gifts as well.

Thyme *(Thymus* spp.*)*

Like basil, there are a huge number of thyme varieties on the market, yet only a few worth growing for the kitchen. Thyme is a woody perennial that can be prostrate (crawls along the ground) or upright. For cooking purposes I prefer the upright thymes, as it is easy to grab a handful and snip the whole lot off with scissors. English thyme or mother-of-thyme are two common names for the basic upright green thyme that has great flavor for your recipes.

Lemon thyme *(T. citriodorus)*, has a distinctly lemon scent as well as taste. Varieties have either glossy green leaves or variegated leaves that are yellow with a dark green border. Lemon thyme can be purchased as a ground cover or an upright plant – and, again, for cooking I prefer the upright versions.

To use fresh thyme, pick the stems and run your fingers down the sides of the stem, from the top to the base, to strip the individual leaves. For casseroles and long-cooking recipes, the whole stems can be thrown into the pot and retrieved before serving. Thyme (zones 5-9) dries well and retains some flavor when frozen.

Drying Herbs

Most herbs dry reasonably well. They should be picked when they are not in flower. Pick a small group of stems and secure them with a string or band, label the group and hang in a cool, dry area away from light – a bedroom closet or basement work well for drying. You can also dry in a dehydrator, but slow drying by hanging retains a little more of the flavor. Always label the herbs, as it is surprising how similar they look when they have dehydrated!

1 teaspoon of dried herbs is equal to 1 tablespoon of fresh herbs.

Here are three basic herb mixes. You should dry the herbs separately before assembling them in roughly equal parts:

- Herbes de Provence: Bay, thyme, marjoram and savory, plus any other Mediterranean herbs that you enjoy – including lavender, which is often added to this mix.

- Fines herbes: a mix of well-scented herbs, such as thyme, chives, rosemary and parsley.

- Bouquet garni: Bay, thyme and parsley, plus other herbs depending on the recipe. Tie the bundle together and add to the pot. Remove before serving.

Making Herb Vinegars

Not all herbs retain their flavor when dried or frozen, but make excellent candidates for herb vinegars. Use a good grade of white wine vinegar and put about an ounce of rinsed and dried-off herbs into a quart of vinegar. Smaller quantities for a standard, off-the-shelf vinegar bottle would be 10 or 12 stems. Pour the contents of the bottle into another vessel and put the fresh herbs into the empty bottle. Refill with vinegar, cap and store in a cool, dark place. Store for about 6 weeks, by which time most of the oils from the herbs have been extracted. Pour the vinegar off into a clean bottle and add a fresh herb stem for decoration. Use herb vinegars directly on salad in summer or when a slight herbal scent is needed in recipes.

4 popular mixes:

- **Chive blossom:** Turns the vinegar a pretty pink and has an oniony flavor.
- **Tarragon:** A classic vinegar used in European recipes.
- **Basil:** A way to get that true basil flavor in winter. Red basils turn the vinegar ruby red.
- **Mint and Rosemary:** One of the few strong-flavored herb vinegars that does well in red wine vinegar.

You can also create customized herb mixes especially for salad dressings or to impart mixed herbal flavors to your casseroles. *Note:* Making herb vinegars is generally considered to be safe – but this is NOT true for herb oils, which need to be processed at very high pressure to kill contaminates.

Herbs to flavor sugar and salt. Just as herbs can add flavor to vinegars, they can also add flavor to sugar and salt. For these, take a large pinch of fresh herb such as lavender and secure in a loose cheesecloth bag. Put a layer of sugar or salt into a non-plastic container (glass or pottery work well) then place the herb on top. Finish with another layer of sugar/salt. Seal the container with a well-fitting lid and place in a dark cupboard for 5 or 6 weeks. As the aromatic herb dries, it imparts the flavor to the dried salt or sugar. Remove the now-dry herb and use the salt or sugar in recipes. You can also chop the fresh herb and mix that in with sugar or salt and dry that way. The dried herb in this case is part of the salt and not removed.

- **Lavender sugar:** Works well when sprinkled on top of vanilla cookies.
- **Sage-flavored salt:** Works well sprinkled on pork chops on the grill.

Tip: Add chopped fresh herbs to butter to give extra flavor to a baked potato. ∎

Growing Fruit in a Small Garden

Now that you have your custom-sized veggie garden organized for healthy suppers, what about a few berries to put on your morning cereal… or maybe a homegrown peach to add to your lunch box? Your garden or patio can take advantage of some new container-sized fruit varieties.

Growing fruit is not too different from growing vegetables, except they are primarily perennials or trees rather than annuals. Like the rest of the garden, your fruit needs full sun and a well-drained, high-nutrient mix to grow in. Container-grown fruit is often subject to winter chill requirements, and all northern growers should be aware that roots in containers get colder than roots in the ground – so protection for outdoor containers is important in cold winters.

Fruit Trees

Fruit trees come in a variety of sizes, from full-sized standard trees to semi-dwarf and dwarf – but even a dwarf apple tree can get 8-10 feet high when mature and almost the same in width, making accommodation in a small garden difficult. Add the need that many fruit trees have for a second tree nearby that acts as a pollinator, and you see why many gardeners are reluctant to grow fruit.

The good news. On the plus side, the industry has made an effort to bring to market some much smaller options for gardeners, including columnar apples and double-grafted fruit trees. Multi-grafted trees are available in cherry, peach, pear and apple varieties, which eliminates the need for several individual trees in the garden for pollination purposes. Most of the multi-grafted trees are dwarf size and reach to about 10 feet when mature. You can even get several different varieties of fruit all on one tree – sometimes marketed as a Fruit Salad Tree.

Let's first look at three kinds of fruit trees that make sense for a small garden or patio.

Apple (*Malus domestica*)

This is the most common fruit to find in columnar size (2 feet wide), although they can still grow to 8-10 feet high. The biggest issue with apple trees is that you need another apple tree variety to pollinate, meaning that they have to bloom at the same time, but – on the plus side – you do get two types of apple. This is true even for the columnar apples, though some companies do a double graft

of compatible trees. Grow the colonnade trees in a small garden bed or containers that are about 24 inches across – the trees are small but the root system does need room to grow.

Citrus

In warmer areas you will see small citrus trees for sale at the garden center in spring. The rest of us go the Internet route to acquire the trees. Whichever way you get the tree, you will be rewarded with fresh oranges, lemons, limes and other great citrus treats. The trees are usually grown in containers because even the slightest frost will kill them, which is why most of us bring the trees indoors for the winter. All citrus are good candidates for pruning to keep small while still bearing fruit each summer. The highly scented white flowers usually arrive early in the year and the resulting fruit takes several months to mature, so be patient.

Plant the young tree in a good container mix. During the growing season, spring and summer, fertilize every two months with a nitrogen-rich fertilizer to keep it healthy. Keep the moisture level even and do not let the container dry out, even in the winter. When you move the plant indoors for winter and outside again in spring, it will need a few days to acclimate to the outdoor environment, just as you do with seedlings. Indoors, the container needs full sun, and although it will be dormant in winter light, it still requires as much light as possible. In frost-free areas, the standard trees can reach to about 12-15 feet high and across. Smaller dwarf trees, averaging 8-10 feet tall, are much more manageable in container and still produce full-size fruits.

Peach *(Prunus persica)*

Peaches are a grown in many areas of North America, but there are different varieties for the cold northern winters and those that prefer only a few cold nights. Always check the growing zones for your choice of peach tree. Most of the trees are available in dwarf size and most are self-pollinating, so you can grow just a single tree. The biggest issue with peach trees in the middle to northern areas is the occurrence of late frosts that arrive after the bloom has begun and the peach is just starting to form. The late frost will not kill the tree and it is unlikely that the leaves on the tree will be killed, yet just one or two degrees of frost can kill the prospect of harvest. But don't despair: you can also find peach trees in colonnade form, which makes protecting the fruit much easier.

Blueberries *(Vaccinium* spp.*)*

Blueberries are the perfect edible landscape shrub because even if you don't want the fruit, they are a three-season-interest shrub. In spring, the bush puts out attractive white bell-shaped flowers that turn into the blueberries. In fall, the foliage turns bright orange and is as colorful as any non-edible shrub in your landscape . And there are native blueberries too. Blueberries can be planted in among the perennial bed or used as hedge material, but can also be grown in container. Blueberries are hardy to zone 4; container varieties are probably zone 4 but that has not really been established yet.

Standard blueberries grow to about 4 or 5 feet tall and wide, with lots to choose from. Northern growers should opt for Northern Highbush varieties, whereas warmer areas grow Southern Highbush or Rabbit Eye blueberry. The container varieties are hardy to about zone 4, but you'll want to give your containers a little extra protection in harsh winters. Many blueberries will produce without a pollinator; however, you will get a larger crop if you have two plants. For a new twist in blueberries look for the variety called Pink Lemonade, which produces a pink berry.

Grapes *(Vitis* spp.*)*

If you have a fence around the garden or can put up a little trellis, then you can probably grow your own grapes. Vines do not grow outward and are easy to

train onto a wire either going up or laterally along a fence. The biggest problem with growing grapes is the tendency for the birds to get the grapes before you do! Pruning grape vines helps keep them from getting too dense and out of control. Prune the vine when it is dormant in late winter and prune back to just a few branches, with each containing lots of little buds. Adjust the pruning as you see growth arrive and remove any that come forward from the fence.

A dwarf grape vine does not have quite the same issues and sits quietly in containers with just a small trellis to support it. These dwarf grape vines reach about 2 feet high and less than that in width, making this a great option for tight spaces.

Raspberries *(Rubus* spp.*)*

There are several varieties of raspberries, including various shades of red, yellow and black, and all these do well in cold as well as warm winter areas. The traditional raspberry grows to about 4 feet tall and produces runners each year that sprout up around the mother cane, which is why raspberries can go wild in just a year or two unless you take a firm hand to keep them tidy. Most raspberries bloom on last year's wood, so the bright green stems that are growing this year will be the ones to bear fruit next year. A few varieties bloom on new wood, making them easier to control by cutting down each year, and some fruit on both old wood for spring harvest and new wood for a late summer harvest. Alas, the berry patch becomes messy, because the prickly

new stems do not stay close to the parent, and each spring I spend a day digging most of them out. The bushes can be corralled onto a stake, but even this takes time to keep the suckers from springing up everywhere. **Contain them!** Growing raspberries in containers does help control this tendency to spread into the surrounding area. There are also dwarf container raspberries that are not only thornless but make a neat form in the container. The dwarf varieties available right now are limited and the harvest is modest, but for a small garden or patio this is a great option. Plant it in a wide container – about 2 feet wide – and give it full sun.

Rhubarb *(Rheum rhabarbarum)*

This is not a tidy plant, but if you enjoy rhubarb, just one or two plants are all you need. They are very easy to grow and do not take up a lot of room, so if your small property has a back corner in sunshine, rhubarb can fill it perfectly. While it does well on the patio in a container, rhubarb would probably be a little too wide for most balconies. Each spring, the bright red stems come out with large, dark green leaves. After a few weeks of harvesting the stems, the plant puts out a flower stalk that can rise to about 4 feet and is quite dramatic! To continue harvesting through the summer, though, I prefer to sever the flower stalk before it gets too tall. The first harvest of rhubarb is usually around the same time as strawberries; they make a great combination in the kitchen.

Strawberries *(Fragaria* hybrids*)*

Strawberries have long been grown in containers and hanging baskets, which tells me that everyone can grow their own strawberries! Each little plant produces flowers and then berries; most varieties flower in spring, making the strawberry the earliest fruit in the garden. Some varieties do repeat bloom all summer, giving you sporadic strawberries all year long. The plants send out runners which, when they touch the ground, root and produce another plant, so you can increase your patch very quickly. Taking out some of the runners to keep the plants in-bounds is simple to do.

Strawberries are very easy to grow in a shallow container as well as a variety of hanging arrangements. Give the plants full sun and make sure to water them often so they don't dry out. You might need to cover the plants as the berries develop to stop birds pecking at them. To keep the berries from resting on the ground where they can rot before they ripen, put a layer of straw on the strawberry patch. ■

PART THREE

THE VEGGIE GARDEN GROWING YEAR:

PLANT BY PLANT, SEASON BY SEASON

EIGHT

Spring

Spring is the start of the growing season. The first sign of warm weather brings out spring fever in us all. Depending on where you are, spring can start as early as February or as late as April. Even with these dates, Mother Nature often throws us a curve ball with extra cold or unusually warm days.

When can I start to plant? A more practical way to look at spring is to take note of how dry and cold the soil is – traditionally indicated by picking up a handful of soil and squeezing it. If it crumbles, the soil is ready to plant, but if it drips water and clumps together, you will need to wait a while until it crumbles.

The earliest vegetables to go directly into the garden are pea seeds and onion sets. Joining them would be transplants of the cool weather kales, chards and salad greens. If you can get these into the ground in March (in warmer areas) or April (cooler areas), there is a good chance that you will have a flourishing crop before the heat of summer kicks in.

Beets *(Beta vulgaris)*

Dark beet globes form under the surface, are easy to grow and do not need the depth of carrots, making them fine for containers as well as raised garden beds. The whole plant is used, both the leafy green leaves and root. Owing to the bright red mid-vein and light green leaves, beets make an attractive feature in the garden. They enjoy cool weather, and they will be finished and out of the garden in time for the tomatoes and warm weather crops.

When to start: Early spring as soon as the soil is dried out. Great winter crop for Southern growers. Direct sow rather than starting indoors.

Care: Easy to grow and frost tolerant.

Fertilizer: An addition of compost to the bed before the seeds are sown is all that you need to do.

Harvest: Baby beets are harvested when the tops are just showing above the surface – when they are about 2 inches across. Mature beets are harvested at about 3 inches in diameter. Baby beets are ready to eat in under 50 days, larger mature beets about 65-70 days.

Store: Can be stored in the soil under a protected mulch or in a cold frame, all winter long. Inside, keep the beets cold and store up to a week.

Preserve: Can or freeze

Varieties: Most beets are dark red (Detroit Dark Red) with some white (White Detroit) or yellow (Golden) varieties.

Cabbages *(Brassica)*

Cabbages can get enormous and be big enough to serve a large family picnic, but they can also be much smaller and great for small gardens. The average supermarket cabbage is about 2-3 lbs., with the plant fitting into a single square foot, but smaller container varieties are available, which are closer to 1 lb. and great for window boxes as well as smaller containers.

When to start: Mild winter area growers can sow the seed directly in the garden or container in early spring. Those of us in the snowbelt are better off starting cabbages indoors about 6-8 weeks before that last frost date.

Store: Cabbage can be stored in the refrigerator for a few weeks.

Preserve: Cabbage does not freeze well, but it can be preserved as sauerkraut (pickled).

Varieties: Most cabbages are green, but you can get red/purple colors too. Heads can be perfectly round or more oval in shape. Both Little Jade and Pixie are container-size cabbages.

Carrots *(Daucus carota)*

Carrots are perfect for both containers and small gardens. You can grow 8-12 per square foot depending on variety. More critical than lateral space is the depth factor. Most small gardens are less than 10 inches deep, so pick a short variety such as a Half Danver or one of the round varieties. Carrots hold well in the garden and can be planted for a fall/winter garden too.

When to start: Carrots cannot be started indoors, so put the seed directly into the ground a week or two before the last frost. Sow the first square or area, then every two weeks after that put a few more in. This way you get a long harvest of sweet carrots. For fall and winter harvest, start sowing seed in mid-July (August for Southern and Western gardens).

Care: As the seedlings grow, remove those that are too close to each other. Small carrots for salads and snacks can be pulled as the plants grow so that the remaining ones have a little more room to develop. Final spacing of about 2 inches is good.

Transplant: Seedlings with at least two real leaves can be planted into a cold frame a week or two before the last frost date – or around the last frost date into the garden.

Care: Cabbage butterflies attack the cabbages almost from the first day that you put them out, so cover them to stop eggs being laid and caterpillars eating the little cabbages before you.

Fertilizer: A good garden bed with compost is great for cabbage, and small ones rarely need extra fertilizer.

Harvest: When the heads are firm and round. Cut the plant from under the leaves and strip the loose outer leaves away. 60-80 days for smaller varieties.

Carrots also can be attacked by a root fly, which is particularly around for early sowing of the crop. Three deterrent suggestions: Put a barrier of cloth over the emerging carrots to stop the fly from landing and laying eggs, inter-plant with onions or marigolds to stop the fly from finding your carrots, or use crop rotation (see page 58).

Fertilizer: Since the carrot root is the part you need, a little fertilizer as it develops is helpful but not essential.

Harvest: Smaller carrots can be removed about 45 days after sowing, while mature carrots are ready 60-70 days after sowing.

Store: Carrots store well in a refrigerator for several weeks. They also store well in a protected garden bed – cover with a heavy layer of straw to insulate from snow and cold.

Preserve: Freeze or can.

Varieties: Look for half-long varieties, like Half Danver, and those with words such as Baby in them. These all work well in shallow garden beds or containers. Colors vary from the common orange to white, yellow and even purple.

Celery *(Apium graveolens)*

Celery is a great addition to salads and recipes, and each takes up only a small amount of ground. They do take a while to mature though, so in very small gardens consider if you want to grow this or not.

When to start: Start indoors about 6 weeks before your last frost date. Celery takes much longer to germinate than most summer vegetables (12-20 days). Can be direct sown into the ground too.

Transplant: After last frost, transplant the seedlings into the garden about 8 inches apart or 2 per square foot.

Care: Traditionally, to get a blanched, paler celery, heap up the soil around them, or plant in a

trench and carefully fill in as the plants get bigger. Inner stems are generally pale green, though, without any attention from the gardener.

Fertilizer: Celery appreciates a good dose of fertilizer about halfway through the growing stage, at about the 30-40 day point.

Harvest: Celery should be a good green color but not too dark. Over-mature stems are bitter. Harvest stalks from the outside as the plant grows or cut the whole plant when the outer stems turn from pale green to a slightly darker green color. Harvest at 75-90 days.

Store: Celery holds up well in the refrigerator for a week or two.

Preserve: Freeze or dry.

Varieties: Most are green, with a few that look more red in color. Tango and Conquistador are two green varieties.

Kale *(Brassica oleracea)*

Kales are some of the hardiest vegetables for both early spring and late summer. They tolerate frost well and come in a variety of different colors, textures and sizes. Colors range from mid-green to blue-green. The leaves, which are crinkled in Scotch kales, can be as small as 6 inches long in dwarf varieties or as large as a foot long for Dinosaur and other large varieties.

When to start: Start inside about 8 weeks before the last frost. In the cool winter areas, sow the kale seeds in winter and let them grow happily in the cool, late winter weather.

Transplant: Even the smallest kales can tolerate some frost and can be hardened off, then planted into the ground about a month before the last frost date.

Care: Kale is part of the cabbage group, but is rarely attacked by butterflies and other insects, in part because of the cool weather that they enjoy. Be vigilant, though, as late winter turns to spring and more insects arrive in the garden.

Fertilizer: A well-composted garden bed is all that kale needs as far as fertilizer goes.

Harvest: Harvest young kale leaves when they are about 4 inches long – at about 45 days. You will need quite a large handful to produce a side dish; it cooks down dramatically.

Store: Fresh leaves can be kept in the cool part of the refrigerator for a few days.

Preserve: Kale leaves can be dried.

Varieties: Scotch kales, like Dwarf Blue Vates; Russian kales, like Dwarf Siberian Kale

Lettuce *(Lactuca sativa)* and Mesclun

Lettuce is one of the easiest vegetables to grow in containers, and it is a great one to start with. Colors range from red to light green with heads from soft and loose to tight Iceberg varieties. There are also those that don't form a head at all. All are suitable for small gardens and containers. Mescluns are usually a mix of "cut and come again" varieties similar to leaf lettuce, but include mustard greens and other spicy leaves.

When to start: Lettuce can be started as seeds to go into the ground about 3-4 weeks before your last frost date – lettuce enjoys cool weather but not frost. It can also be started indoors for transplanting in spring. For containers that you can drag indoors: If the spring weather changes to cold nights, you can start lettuce much earlier – about 8 weeks before your last frost. In mild areas, sow seed indoors in late winter and transplant seedlings in early spring.

Transplant: When the seedlings have two sets of true leaves, harden them off a few days, then plant the seedlings in a protected bed in mid to late spring. Cover if light frosts are likely.

Store: Lettuce will keep fresh in the refrigerator for a few days.

Preserve: Lettuce does not preserve well.

Varieties: There are numerous varieties and they all work well in the garden. Look for cool weather ones for northern springs, and varieties that tolerate warm weather for the summer. Return to cool weather lettuce varieties in the fall. Lettuce also holds up well in a cold frame and will return and grow much earlier than you expect!

Onions and Garlic *(Allium)*

Onions come in a variety of sizes that range from small scallions through the wonderful shallots and all the way up to large Vidalia-style onions. They are also divided into short and long day length – northern long days spur the onion to form, whereas in the South where the day length is not as long, a mid-day variety is preferred. There are also some short-day varieties for Southern growers to grow in late winter or early spring.

When to start: Onion seed should be started very early in the year so that it gets large enough to transplant in spring. Larger containers would be fine for garlic; small onions such as scallions do well in containers as well as small gardens.

Transplant: Onion sets and garlic cloves are put directly into the ground or container.

Care: Garlic and onion are rarely attacked by insects or even deer in the garden. They can, however, suffer from maggots that attack the roots and developing bulb, and thrips (tiny black insects) on the stem.

Fertilizer: Needs only a good, loose soil with plenty of compost.

Harvest: Small scallions can be harvested as soon as they form a small bulb. Larger bulbs for onions take a while to form (60-90 days) but should be ready in early summer. The top growth starts to turn brown when the bulbs are mature.

Store: Mature bulbs can be stored for several months in a dark, dry location. Brush the dirt off the bulb and let it dry completely outside before bringing indoors to store.

Preserve: Chop and dry, pickle.

Varieties: Scallions and shallots are smaller varieties of onion. Walla-Walla, Candy and Texas Supersweet are more traditional-size bulbs.

Peas *(Pisum sativum)*

Peas are a vining plant that can be planted early in the year. Vines range from container-size at just a couple of feet long to those that reach over 7 feet. Some varieties have pods that are edible; with others, you wait until the pod is full of tender peas. Pea tendrils can also be eaten. Peas do take some room, though, and in a small garden that should be taken into consideration. It does, however, grow and produce early in the year and is usually out of the garden before the beans need to go in. Peas can also be planted for a late season crop. Peas come in a variety of different-colored pods and flowers, ranging from purple through green to bright yellow!

When to start: As soon as the ground is warm in spring. Ground that is too cold and frozen rots the seed, but you do need to be prompt so that the pods have time to mature. For colder areas, start in March/April; in warmer climates, as early as late February. Peas, and beans benefit from being planted with an inoculant, which is a combination of bacteria and helps the peas germinate and grow.

Transplant: Sow peas directly where you plan to grow them.

Care: Give peas a support and make sure that you do that at the same time as you sow the seed. In a container on the deck, your deck railing can double as the support; for others, a simple string supported vertically or a chicken wire frame works well.

Fertilizer: Like most early crops, peas do not need much more than a good compost-based soil.

Harvest: Snow peas are harvested when the pods are well-formed and green, but the peas are still tiny. The snap peas have edible pods with small peas formed inside. The main crop of shelling peas are harvested when the pods are full, with well-formed peas inside. Most snap peas mature earlier than main crop, allowing a long pea season. To use the edible tendrils (Masterpiece, particularly, has very attractive tendrils): When the peas get to about 2 feet high, harvest the tendrils by cutting them back to around 6 inches. The peas regrow very quickly to flower and yield a crop of great shelling peas.

Store: Peas are best eaten fresh from the garden, but can be stored a day or two in the cool part of the refrigerator.

Preserve: Freeze, dry or can.

Varieties: Super Sugar Snap; Dwarf Grey Sugar Snow Pea; Peas-in-a-Pot, Bantam Dwarf (shelling peas); Masterpiece.

Spinach *(Spinacia oleracea)*

Spinach is easy to grow in spring and matures in a matter of a few weeks. Most varieties have mid-green leaves; it is most often lightly stir-fried. Young leaves are added to salads, mature leaves are used in recipes such as quiche.

When to start: Spinach can be started indoors, but does very well outside in cool weather. More important to note is that it does not tolerate hot weather, so has to be given time to mature before summer arrives. Start a few seeds every week or so for a long harvest.

Transplant: As early as possible in spring. Cold frames are great for late winter spinach, even in the North.

Care: Mostly trouble-free, so long as the weather is cool. Most insects are not active this early in the year. When the weather warms up, the spinach starts to bolt and the leaves get bitter, so pull the plant.

Fertilizer: A well-composted bed or cold frame is all spinach needs.

Harvest: When the young leaves are several inches long, for eating raw in salads. Main leaves are 6-7 inches long. Spinach matures in less than 50 days in most cases, with young leaves being harvested as soon as 25 days.

Store: Spinach can be stored in the cool part of the refrigerator for a week or two.

Preserve: Freeze or dry.

Varieties: Crocodile, Salad Fresh, Tyee.

Swiss Chard *(Beta vulgaris* subsp.*)*

The chard of our grandparents is not the colorful vegetable that we find on the market today, although the traditional green leaf with a white core is still available. The seeds are slightly smaller than a pea and they germinate in cool soil in 10-15 days. The immature seed germinates with the bright red or yellow of the mature plant, making an attractive set of seedlings on the shelf. Both leaf and mid-vein are edible, although with more mature stems you will want to strip the leaf, chop the central vein and cook that for a minute or two before you add the leaf.

When to start: Chard is a cool-weather vegetable that can be grown over the winter in mild winter areas. Northern area gardeners start the seeds indoors for about 6 weeks.

Transplant: A week or two before the last frost is a good time to move chard into the garden, but keep a cloth handy if a really cold night occurs. Cold frames are perfect for these early vegetables.

Care: Chard is very easy to grow and rarely needs more care than just watching to see that the groundhog doesn't get them.

Fertilizer: A nice layer of compost before the seedlings are transplanted is a good idea, but no further fertilization is needed.

Harvest: Harvest when the young leaves are 4-8 inches long. Mature leaves are darker and have a stronger mid-stem which can be removed if you want to, or just stir-fry it a little longer than the leaves. A mix of white, red and yellow stems makes for a colorful side dish.

Store: Store in a cool vegetable drawer for a day or two.

Preserve: Dry or freeze.

Varieties: Colorful stems can be found on chard with names like Neon Lights, Rainbow and Bright Lights. ■

Summer

Regardless of the calendar and weatherman, for gardeners the summer begins with the average last frost date. This magic date is an average date for the last frost for your locality, in the two weeks before you have progressively less and less chance of a frost. This does not mean, however, that you can dive right in and plant all those hot weather plants! Some years the ground is warm and days are consistently in the 80s with nights in the upper 50s, while other years the temperatures hover in the mid 50s with night temperatures in the low 40s. In these cool but frost-free days you can plant beans, but it is better to wait another week or two before planting the real summer crops such as tomatoes, peppers, squash, sweet corn and basil.

Beans *(Phaseolus vulgaris)*

All varieties of beans grow in a similar way. Traditional green beans and slender French beans (also called filet or haricot vert) enjoy hot summer days, whereas the pretty red flowering runner beans enjoy the slightly cooler temperatures of early summer and fall. Beans that are intended for drying also grow well in summer temperatures, but wait until the beans have dried on the vine before harvesting. They take a lot of space in small gardens, so unless you really want to try to grow your own kidney beans, it's best to keep to the other varieties.

All bean varieties germinate better if they are planted with an inoculant. This is sold under a number of names and is a black powder containing bacteria that benefit the growth of beans (and peas). I moisten the beans in a baggie with a little compost tea (see page 53), then toss in a teaspoon or so of inoculant. Shake to distribute the powder, then plant.

When to start: Beans are started directly in the garden. I like to try to start them a week or two before the last frost date – but I do check the 10-day forecast before I do that. The first to go in are the runner beans, with the French and pole beans a week later. Beans are a great plant for succession planting – just do a few seeds each week for several weeks to get a long harvest.

Care: Most beans need a trellis in place before they start to grow. Vines range from just a few feet right up to 7 or 8 feet! This is fine if your deck can double as a trellis; otherwise, provide a tall structure. Teepee-like structures are popular for beans, and beans are part of the Three Sisters planting where the corn stalks support the beans (see page 78). Watch for a speckled beetle called the Mexican bean beetle. This pest looks like an oversized striped ladybug, and she puts her eggs on the underside of the leaves. Check regularly and deal with the beetle by spraying a horticultural soap onto the eggs and dumping the beetles into a jug of soapy water.

Fertilizer: Beans, like peas, contribute nitrogen to the ground, but I do add a little extra fertilizer to the bed before the beans are planted and again when the flowers are being produced.

Harvest: French beans are harvested when they are barely as thick as a pencil; harvest traditional beans when a little thicker but still around the diameter of a pencil. (Pole beans are traditional green beans with long vines, whereas the bush beans are more compact.) Runner beans and those with bright red or pink blossoms are flatter and broader than most beans. They also have a fuzzy covering. Harvest these beans when the bean inside is just starting to swell. Harvest beans anywhere from 55-75 days.

Store: Beans are much better eaten within a day of harvest.

Preserve: Green beans can be frozen and canned. Kidney/navy beans are dried when picked; store in the freezer.

Varieties: Tom Thumb, dwarf bush beans.

Eggplant *(Solanum melongena)*

Eggplants are known as aubergines in Europe and are part of the potato family. They need warm to hot temperatures to grow and produce attractive blossoms. Most eggplants are 4-6 inches long and a broad oval in shape. Colors vary from light speckled pink to dark shiny purple. Most plants grow to about 3 feet tall and will work in containers. There are some new, smaller varieties that produce much smaller fruit.

When to start: Eggplants take a long time to mature, so starting indoors 6 weeks or so before your last frost date is a good idea. The seeds are large and germinate in about 10 days in a warm room. Make a second sowing of seeds directly in the ground a week or two after the last frost so that you get a long supply for the kitchen.

Transplant: Seedlings can be planted outdoors after the danger of frost and the soil is warm.

Care: These attractive plants are easy to grow and rarely suffer from problems unless they are cold. Cool and damp summers can lead to wilts and fungus issues, so don't rush the plants outside. Raised beds and containers warm up slightly faster and are great options for growing eggplants. Provide a support for the plants too, as a mature plant can have 10 or 15 fruit maturing at the same time.

Fertilizer: Add a good compost before you plant eggplants and a dose of fertilizer about a month after you plant them.

Harvest: The fruit should be a consistent color throughout but not soft. Eggplants mature in 50-75 days depending on variety.

Store: Eggplants can be stored in the refrigerator for a few days.

Preserve: Peel and freeze; dry.

Varieties: Fairy Tale (small striped purple fruit); Patio Baby (small purple fruit); Orlando (small purple fruit).

Melons *(Cucurbitaceae)*

Melons are a summer favorite everywhere, but because of their large, sprawling vines and the long time it takes them to produce fruit, they are not ideal for the very small garden or container. The vines can be corralled onto a support fence; however, the heavy melon fruit, particularly watermelon, needs to be accommodated as well as the vine. There is a "melon cradle" that keeps the fruit off the ground, though it's not a support for plants in a container. Fruits vary in size from soccer ball size in musk and honeydew melons to much larger for watermelons. A few melon varieties are suitable for containers – just make sure that you have some support close by.

When to start: Like many summer crops, just being frost-free is not good enough for melon seeds to germinate. They like warm soil. Sow just 1 or 2 seeds in a hill in the garden and wait for the large leaves to erupt.

Care: Melons grow quickly. As long as you have something for them to crawl over they are reasonably easy to care for. They need plenty of water to create the lush, moist fruit; some sources suggest less water when the fruit is almost ripe in order to make the melon sweeter.

Fertilizer: Start with a rich soil, with a dose of fertilizer once the plants develop the second set of leaves and take off running.

Harvest: The melons sound "hollow" when you knock on them if they are ripe. The base should be able to be depressed just a little, and the melon will detach from the vine without too much trouble – you will probably still need a knife though.

Store: Melons store well in a cool area, but once cut they should be used within a few days.

Preserve: Melons do not can or dry well. Melon balls can be frozen.

Varieties: Ice Box and Sugar Baby watermelons; Muskateer (honeydew); Inspire (Cantaloupe).

Okra *(Abelmoschus esculentus)*

You only need one or two plants for an abundant supply of okra! The attractive plants are part of the mallow family and have a very pretty bloom, making them popular for front yard gardens too. The fruit are formed and mature almost overnight, and the plants have little spikes on them, so take care when cultivating around them. Most varieties are below 4 feet tall with little width, making them fine for small gardens and containers.

When to start: Start seed indoors in northern areas and sow directly outdoor in warmer areas, after the danger of frost has passed.

Transplant: Okra is available as a small plant as well as seed and should be planted outside when the weather has settled to summer temperatures. Space them about one per foot.

Care: Once the plants are established, okra grows with very little trouble.

Fertilizer: A light fertilizer when planted is all it needs to produce lots of fruit.

Harvest: The prolific production of okra means that you pick every day once they start producing. The pods should be about 4 inches long and barely as broad as your thumb. They become woody and tasteless if they are left longer, but the over-ripe pods can be dried and strung together for creative crafters to use in wreaths and floral arrangements!

Store: Okra does store a day or two, but as more is ripe outside, it is best to use it straight away.

Preserve: Can, freeze or dry.

Varieties: Bull Dog (around 3 feet), Baby Bubba (container size).

Okra flowers are especially appealing in the garden.

Peppers *(Capsicum)*

Peppers come in a number of different sizes and shapes, with "heat" ranging from sweet to very hot. All are great for containers and small gardens and enjoy the heat of summer. Like eggplants, start seeds indoors and do not rush the pepper outside until the temperature is consistently in the 80s and nights are above 60 degrees. The heat factor of peppers is rated on the Scoville Scale, where the higher the number the more heat you will get in your recipe.

When to start: Peppers germinate quickly and can be started within a month of the last frost date. If you can provide a heat mat underneath the seed, try it; you will get much faster germination, since they like warm soil.

Transplant: The weather should be settled into a summer pattern for peppers. Transplant them when they have at least 4 true leaves. It is much better to keep the peppers in a container on the deck until summer arrives than to rush it into the garden while the temperature swings can bring cool nights.

Care: Peppers need full sun and the hotter the better! Consistent water is necessary but peppers usually don't get too many issues with bugs except the occasional aphids, which are easy to rinse off.

Fertilizer: Transplant peppers into a fertile soil and add a second dose of fertilizer as the plants grow.

Harvest: Most hot peppers are harvested when the fruit is bright red. Sweet and milder peppers range from green through yellow to red. Note the days to maturity on the seed package to get an idea of when to harvest and what color to expect.

Store: The whole peppers hold up well in the refrigerator for about a week. Once cut, they should be used with 2 days.

Preserve: Dry or freeze.

Varieties: Most peppers are great in containers, so all you have to do is find out which one works best for your palate.

Sweet Corn (Zea mays)

Sweet corn has been grown in large gardens for ages. Until recently, it has taken a lot of room to get the complete pollination required for a decent crop. That has changed in the last few years, and a 10x10-foot garden is no longer needed. However, it is still a good idea to grow in a group rather than a single line. Look for varieties that do not get much above 5 feet high and space the seeds about a foot apart. You will harvest 2 or 3 ears per stalk in about 2 months. As sweet corn does take a long while, it is best to reserve a 4x4-foot bed just for the corn over the summer or a container for your crop. This way you can still have room for tomatoes and other great crops. Or, you can do a traditional Three Sisters planting (see page 78) with corn, beans and summer squash. Be sure to plant where the corn's height will not shade other summer crops.

When to start: Sweet corn is sown directly into warm soil, around the same time as you plant peppers and summer squash.

Care: Keep the garden well-weeded while the young corn grows. It does, however, look like grass as it germinates, so I like to let it get to about 6 inches tall before getting all the grass-like weeds out. Corn does not need to be supported but can be used to support other plants.

Fertilizer: Sweet corn is a heavy feeder. Give a dose of fertilizer when the plants are about 6 inches tall and again in about a month into the growing season.

Harvest: Sweet corn is a long-growing crop, but worth the wait! Each ear will fill out with little sweet corn seeds. Harvest when the seeds at the top are plump and juicy.

Store: Ears can be stored a few days, but are much better eaten within a day of harvest.

Preserve: Shuck and freeze, dry or can.

Varieties: Look for varieties that grow to about 5 feet at most. On Deck and Early Sunglow are both varieties that top out at about 4 feet and can be grown in containers.

Summer Squash (Cucurbita)

Summer squash plants are large, sprawling and very prolific! Most people get rather inundated with summer squash; the best method is to plant just one seed every other week so that you have a steady but not overwhelming supply. Summer squash can be grown in a container, but make sure you have room for it to roam a little. Squash puts out two sorts of flowers, a female one and a male one. The bright yellow male flowers arrive as much as a week before the plant starts putting out female flowers (see photo on page 58).

When to start: Squash like warm soil, so start planting when you transplant your peppers.

Transplant: Although you can start the seeds indoors, they grow quickly, and most people just sow the seeds directly into the soil outside. If you do decide to start indoors, sow just one or two weeks before the last frost. I like to make a little hill for the seed – the soil warms up quicker in a small hilled area.

Care: Squash can be attacked by several problems. Squash beetles and borers are by far the most common and they can fell a plant overnight. Look for areas of the stem near the ground that have turned to mush. Sometimes with a very vigorous plant it will just continue to grow, but smaller plants do not last long after the borers attack them. Supporting the vines on a trellis helps keep the borers out of the stem (they climb up from the ground). A less deadly issue is mildew on the large leaves. Moist, humid air creates a great environment for fungus and mold. If just one leaf is affected by mildew, go ahead and remove the leaf. When the majority of the leaves are covered, the overall health of the plant is affected. In this case, you can treat the issue easily with an organic fungicide. Summer squash also has issues with pollination – it takes many pollinator visits to the female flower for it to successfully pollinate the plant. This is most noticeable in

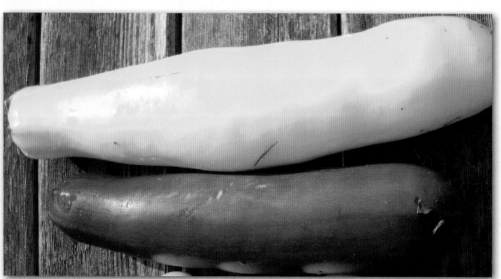

completely, you will have plenty to harvest. Look for even color and well-rounded shape along the length of the squash. Incomplete fertilization leads to a small fruit that is slightly shriveled at the end. Squash that is ripe will detach easily from the vine.

Varieties: There are many varieties of summer squash, among them the green Black Beauty and the yellow Goldrush. A great option for containers is Patio Star, which produces in as little as 50 days.

the very early season and the late season flowers. For most of the season, once you get started, nature takes care of things very well.

Fertilizer: Squash is a fast growing plant, so give it a good start in well-composted soil. Most plants do not need any further fertilizer.

Harvest: Squash is one of those vegetables that grows from just-started to overripe in what seems like a day. Assuming the flowers were pollinated

Tomatoes *(Solanaceae)*

Tomatoes are probably the most common and rewarding vegetable to grow in the garden. They are nutritious, come in a variety of great tastes and colors and make a great in-the-garden snack straight off the plant! Do not expect your homegrown tomatoes to look like the almost-too-perfect, even, pale red samples from the supermarket, but you can expect great taste and various textures. Some tomatoes are dense with lots of pulp, great for sauces and canning. Others are thin-skinned with lots of juice, perfect for salads. Growing just 2 or 3 plants can give you tomatoes for all your needs. With so many varieties to choose from, it is best to make a list of attributes before you start. If you enjoy pasta with tomato sauce, you will need one of the Italian plum varieties. For salads you might like a medium-sized yellow tomato, and for burgers from the grill, one of the large red varieties.

When to start: Start the tomatoes from seed about 6 weeks before the last frost date. Any earlier and you risk getting straggly plants that attract insects and infections. Plants can be found at many local garden centers, which is a good option too. Again, make sure that you know what characteristics you want before you shop – tomatoes are addictive and you would not be the first person to get carried away and find yourself with 6 or 8 tomato plants!

Transplant: When the seed-grown plants have at least two sets of real leaves, they can be transplanted. Larger seedlings are happy if they are potted up to a larger container for a week or two and held back until the weather is settled. Planting outside, the soil should be warm and the forecast free of frosts. Ideally, the days should be at least mid-70s with lows in the 50s, but they prefer warm 80-degree days with summer nights of mid-60s.

Care: Tomatoes need constant moisture; irrigation insures that the plants get it. Rainy summer weather and inconsistent moisture create tomatoes that have a flattened, black base. Tomatoes do suffer from a few major disease issues that are soil-borne and cause a quick death to the plants. This is more a concern when you grow in the ground and do not rotate the site where you grow tomatoes each year. A way to avoid these issues is by planting a disease-resistant variety in a raised bed with a good planting soil as the base.

Fertilizer: Tomatoes are best planted in a bed that has lots of compost worked in. A dose of fertilizer about a month after planting and again when the flowers are setting keeps the plants producing. A tomato fertilizer has a higher phosphorous content than most for good fruit set.

Harvest: Ripe tomatoes come off the plant very easily; unripe ones do not. This is useful to know if you have forgotten what color your tomato should be when ripe. Green tomatoes can be the final color or it can be an unripe tomato – you would not be the first to wait until the green tomato drops to

realize that this is the color when the fruit is ripe! Small cherry tomatoes are usually the first to ripen, and before long you will have more than enough for your needs.

Store: Tomatoes can be stored for a day or two, depending on the variety.

Preserve: Dry individual tomatoes; freeze or can tomato sauce.

Varieties: Tiny Tom, Patio Princess, Tumbling Tom are all small varieties that can be grown in containers or a small garden. Supersauce and Roma are paste tomatoes.

Tomato Viruses and Other Issues

Tomatoes suffer from a host of problems, but growing in containers and raised beds does help avoid some of the major ones. Look for plants that have TMV, F, V, and A-resistant tags on the label or description.

Tobacco Mosaic Virus: Tomatoes are in the same family as tobacco and suffer from similar issues. Tobacco virus is introduced via cuts on the plant and shows as a mottled green and yellow leaf, plus stunted growth. Clear all debris from last year from the garden, and take care not to break leaves, etc., when you plant the tomato. Resistance is shown by the tag TMV or sometimes just M.

Fusarium wilt: The leaves turn brown and die off from the base and the stem turns brown before the whole plant is affected. Discard the plant and do not compost or grow tomatoes in that spot for a couple of years at least. Resistant varieties are indicated by F1, F2, F3.

Verticillium wilt: Verticillium enters the plant through the root system and shows up as a brown ring inside the branches. Leaves turn brown and wilt quickly. Resistance is noted by V.

Alternaria: This is a canker rather than a virus, but it can kill the plants. The black cankers grow on the stem and leaves, distorting the fruit. Look for A on the tag.

Tomato hornworm: These large caterpillars arrive almost overnight and have enormous appetites for your tomato plant. If unchecked, they can defoliate a plant in hours! There is a little white bug that kills the caterpillar, so if you see little white things sticking out of the worm, it is already dead. If they are alive and eating, I generally trim the whole leaf that it is eating and discard both away from the tomato bed.

Cat Face: A crack develops on the tomato that dries out and looks like a smile. Usually caused by too much water.

Fall and Winter

*F*all gardens really start in mid- to late summer as the days get slowly shorter and night temperatures come down. This is perfect for cool weather vegetables, though the cooler days lead to a slightly longer time for them to mature. Fall is a good time in the vegetable garden; there is more consistent rainfall, the soil is warm and fewer bugs are around to harm your crop. The best crops to grow are those that you started with in spring: the leafy vegetables, carrots and peas. Fast-growing peas and spinach can be sown directly into the ground in late summer (but longer-growing cabbages are best started indoors where the temperatures are slightly cooler).

A little shade is good. August temperature will be very hot in most regions, so pick an area of the garden that has a little bit of shade. The shade may be from other, mature plants. For example, you can start your fall veggies growing under the beans, and by the time the new plants get a little bigger and peep through the beans, the temperature will have moderated and they can enjoy the slightly cooler fall sunshine. An alternate way to offer shade to your plants is to cover them with dark tulle netting from the fabric store.

Keeping them warm as long as possible. As fall progresses and turns into early winter, the first frosty nights arrive. Typically, there will be a few light frosts followed by another week or two of milder weather. This is where covers and cold frames really make the difference. A heavy cloth or simple rigid plastic cover over the bed will keep the temperature just one or two degrees warmer for the plants underneath, and thus they are not felled by the frost. Keeping them alive for one or two chilly nights can give you another two weeks of produce. Carrots, kales and chards will all survive well into the winter if they are fully grown in a simple cold frame. They can be harvested as long as the ground and leaves are not frozen; a sunny winter day usually thaws the cold frame by midday.

Brussels Sprouts

Brussels sprouts are the stars of the fall garden and popular in fall and winter meals. Cold tolerant and very tolerant of frost, they do take a long time to grow, so be prepared to allocate a square for a full 3 months for this fall vegetable.

When to start: Seeds can be started as early as July 4th to give the Brussels time to mature. If you started them indoors or in a seedling tray outside, transplant into the garden when the seedlings have 2 sets of leaves.

Care: Mid-season bugs can be a nuisance with this crop, as it is in the garden for so long, so watch for aphids and caterpillars.

Fertilizer: Fertilize when the seedlings are put out, with a second dose about a month later.

Harvest: The Brussels are produced along the tall stalk. Harvest when they are firm and about an inch in diameter. The whole stalk can be harvested at once, or pick off the individual sprouts starting from the bottom, which mature first. Days to maturity: 100-120.

Store: Brussels sprouts last for a few weeks in the refrigerator and freeze well. Whole stems last a little longer if kept cool.

Preserve: Freeze.

Varieties: Most Brussels sprouts varieties are green (Dimitri and Igor), but Falstaff is purple.

Cabbage

Like the spring cabbage, the small-headed cabbages are great for the fall garden.

When to start: Indoors in mid- to late July, about 3 months before your first fall frost. Transplant the seedlings when they have 2 sets of true leaves, outside in an area of the garden where the hot afternoon sun doesn't bake them.

Care: Seedlings take more water than mature vegetables, so make sure that they don't dry out during the day. Watch for late butterflies, but these are less of a pest in fall than in spring.

Fertilizer: A light, general fertilizer before you plant the seedlings will suffice.

Harvest: When the heads are mature and firm. Days to maturity: 60 -75.

Store: Late cabbages can be stored in a cool area for several weeks.

Preserve: Preserve as sauerkraut.

Varieties: Earliana, Gonzales, Pixie.

Carrots

Carrots can be sown late in the year and they will mature in a few months and be ready for harvest. If you sow some seed in a cold frame you will be able to harvest the carrots all through the winter, or as long as the supply lasts.

When to start: Fall carrots take at least 60 days to mature, so for areas where frost starts in September, you need to start carrots directly where they are to grow – in mid-July at the latest.

Care: Protect the mature carrots at the end of the season with a cloth or straw to extend the harvest.

Fertilizer: Fertilize the area just before or when you sow the seed.

Harvest: As long as the ground is not frozen, you can harvest when mature. As for summer carrots, thin the seedlings to about 2 inches apart so that the root has room to grow. Days to maturity: 65-70.

Store: In a refrigerator the carrots last a few weeks. In the ground they will last most of the winter.

Preserve: Can or freeze.

Varieties: Touchon, Caracas

Garlic

Garlic is great when planted in fall. The little cloves are planted along with fall bulbs, but they put up the first shoots in late fall. Even when covered with snow, the garlic persists and when the late winter thaw arrives, they start growing again. This gives them a major advantage against the cloves that are planted in spring, which will not be ready until much later in summer. For a long harvest, you can add a few spring garlic bulbs when you plant the spring onions.

When to plant: Late September through early November, depending on your region. I like to plant the cloves after the first frost has cooled the ground.

Care: The bulbs are wonderfully easy to care for. Even in cold winters they survive.

Harvest: Harvest in early to midsummer when the top of the green stems start to turn brown.

Days to maturity: 150+ for spring planted garlic, a little longer for those that are started in fall and pause for the winter.

Store: Dry the whole bulb before storing in a cool place where it will store for several months.

Preserve: Dry.

Varieties: Hard neck garlic and soft neck garlic are the two major divisions. The hard neck are more cold tolerant, whereas the soft neck are better for southern regions.

Kale

Kales are very cold tolerant and will do fine in fall frosts. In fact, they are said to improve after a few frosty nights!

When to start: Start the seeds indoors in late July. A few seeds in the ground in mid-August also works. Transplant when the seedlings have 2 sets of leaves. I like to plant them in an area that is shaded from hot afternoon sun.

Care: Watch for stress in the seedlings if the weather is still hot outside. They grow slowly in warm weather and will put a spurt on when the temperature drops.

Fertilizer: A light dose when planting is all you need.

Harvest: Harvest when the leaves are several inches long. Just like spring kale, these regrow happily when you harvest the leaves on a cut-and-come-again basis. Days to maturity: 55-65.

Store: Kale stores well for a few weeks in the cool drawer of the refrigerator.

Preserve: Dry or freeze.

Varieties: Fast-growing Russian kales and Dwarf Blue Vates both mature quickly.

Lettuce

Lettuce is a cool weather crop, but some varieties do well in heat. A variety that transitions from heat to cool fall weather will perform well for you.

When to start: Warm season lettuce can be started by seed throughout the summer and into fall. Change to cool season varieties in August for varieties that will mature in September/October. Warmer areas can stay with heat tolerant varieties longer and grow cold-tolerant varieties for fall and winter.

Care: Stress from hot afternoon sun and lack of water are the main concerns with summer-sown lettuce. Some afternoon shade is great for them when they are small.

Fertilizer: A light dose of nutrients just before you sow the seeds in summer is all that lettuce needs.

Harvest: Harvest on a cut-and-come-again basis when the leaves are 4 inches long. For head lettuce, harvest the whole lettuce plant when the head is

well formed. Days to maturity: leaf lettuce 45-55; head lettuce 65-70.

Store: Lettuce stores for a few days only, so a constant supply is needed.

Preserve: Lettuce does not preserve well.

Varieties: For summer to fall: Heatwave. Late summer to fall: Romaine varieties. The main fall crop: Bibb or leaf lettuce.

Peas

Late season peas are great to round out the garden year. Quick-growing snow and snap peas are faster growers than shelling peas, but in warmer areas you can do both. Remember to use an inoculant with the peas just as you did in spring (see page 128).

When to start: Plant seeds directly in the garden in early August.

Care: Depending on the variety, the pea vines do need support. A bean vine can sometimes offer support to the peas as the beans are winding down in September, and the peas are producing.

Fertilizer: A good compost is the best for peas, or a light fertilizer.

Harvest: Pick the pods when they are just starting to swell with little peas. Days to harvest: 50-70.

Store: Both snow peas and snap peas hold up well in the refrigerator for a few days.

Preserve: Peas can be dried, frozen or canned.

Varieties: Sugar Snap/Super Sugar Snap; Snow Bird, Dwarf White Sugar.

Spinach

Most spinach is ready in about 30 days, which makes it perfect for fall planting. Enjoy it all the way through to frost and beyond.

When to start: Sow seeds directly into the ground from late August. Start a few seeds indoors in mid-August (cooler areas) to late August (warm areas). Transplant any seedlings by early September when they have 2 sets of real leaves.

Fertilizer: Spinach really does not need fertilizer, but a light dose when planting is always a good idea.

Harvest: Harvest young plant leaves for salads and eating fresh. Mature leaves are great steamed or stir-fried. Days to harvest: 35-55.

Store: Store in the cool part of the refrigerator for a week or so.

Preserve: Freeze or dry.

Varieties: Fast growers like Crocodile and Giant work well in fall.

Winter Squash

Winter squash is another vegetable that takes a long time to mature but is great for fall gardens and fall recipes. Like the summer squash, the vines are not frost tolerant, so you need to start these in summer. Several varieties are available and some are more compact than others. Acorn, butternut and spaghetti are the three main types of winter squash.

When to start: Sow seed directly into the ground in late June through July to give these winter vegetables time to mature before the first frosts hit.

Care: Keep the vines well watered in dry weather and through summer. Less water is needed as fall weather arrives and the squash matures.

Fertilizer: A good organic matter to start is important, then a general fertilizer after about 2 months.

Harvest: Give it a gentle tap to test for ripeness; if it sounds hollow, it is ripe. The fruit comes off the vine easily. Days to harvest: 80-100.

Store: Store the squash in a cool area where it will stay healthy for several weeks.

Preserve: Freeze.

Varieties: Tivoli (spaghetti type); Honey Bear (acorn) and Pilgrim (butternut)

APPENDIX

WHAT'S EATING MY PLANTS?

TYPES OF CONTAINERS AND THEIR USES

SOME NATURAL FERTILIZERS AND WHAT THEY DO

What's Eating My Plants?
"Bad Bugs" and Other Undesirables

However carefully you plan your downsized veggie garden, sometimes things go wrong. Some of these problems are due to weather-related conditions, and others are specific to one vegetable only. Problems that are related to just one vegetable, such as the tomato hornworm, are discussed on page 142. Some insects and problems are general and affect multiple plants in the garden; these are classified as insect, animal and mold/fungal problems. Here we look at some of the most common, non-plant-specific issues that you might find.

As with all disease and disease control, it is important that you:

1. Know what you are dealing with and its life cycle.
2. Read the label carefully before you apply a control remedy.

Insect damage: Insects feed on either the tissue of the plant leaf or stem, or they feed on the insects that are doing the damage; so, some insects are the good guys, and some are the bad guys.

Borers

Whereas some insects remain on the surface of the plant, borers bore into the soft stem where they are tough to see. Borers are serious problems on squash, corn and several other vegetables, often compromising the overall health of the plant. Generally, the borers are in the larval stage of development; they consume the tissue of the plant before taking flight to deposit eggs somewhere else. Two good ways to prevent problems: cover plants when they are small and the moths are flying around and check on the plants to spot eggs before borers hatch. Clearly, many vegetables need to be uncovered for pollination, so uncover the plants when the flowers arrive. Putting a cuff of a toilet roll tube around the seedling can also help prevent the moth from depositing eggs on the plant in the first place.

Aphids

These are tiny, usually white insects with 6 legs, and they extract moisture and nutrients from the plant leaves and stem. You may not notice the damage unless you are close up, where you will see a crowd of little guys under the leaf surface. Most aphids do not fly and can be knocked off the plant with a good spray from the hose. To spot these guys, look for a mass of white or light-colored "dots" under a curled-up leaf. Aphids can sometimes be found by following a trail of ants that are attracted to the sticky residue that the aphids left behind.

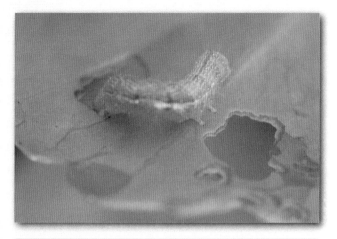

Caterpillars (and cutworms)

From grade school you probably learned that the butterfly starts as an egg, develops into the hungry caterpillar, pupates and become a butterfly again. Most of those phases do not affect your vegetables, but the caterpillar stage most certainly does. Some caterpillars are ones that we really would like to preserve because of the final butterfly, but others we prefer to destroy before they eat their way through the whole cabbage or potato leaf. Damage from caterpillars occurs when they eat the green leaves of your plants, particularly those of the cabbage family. Large holes in the leaves are unsightly, but when whole leaves on young plants are consumed, the damage can kill the plant. Cutworms are also caterpillars. They find tender young seedlings and fell them overnight. The damage from cutworms is at ground level, whereas the caterpillar effectively severs the stems. Reduce cutworm damage by placing a collar from a kitchen roll or other barrier around the seedling until it is big enough to survive. If you remove caterpillars and the egg mass when you see them, and cover spring plants so that the butterfly cannot reach the leaves, you will alleviate the issue. Be vigilant even after you have covered the plants, in case there are eggs already on the leaf and develop into caterpillars, who then eat the plants.

Flea beetle

The damage from the flea beetle is similar to a miniature army firing lots of tiny round pellets through the leaf. They do not skeletonize the leaf, but continued damage can compromise the health of the plant. The beetles can jump effectively from one leaf or plant to another and will do so when you disturb them. Covering the vegetables in early spring is helpful, and removal of the beetles (that appear as dark-colored dots on the leaf) is also possible. For large populations, an organic insecticide, oil or soap might need to be used.

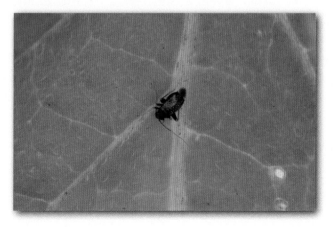

Leaf miners

These are tiny little fly larvae that burrow into the leaf itself. Once inside, it is difficult to extract them without sacrificing the whole leaf. Leaf miners eat the matter between the leaf surfaces, and thus are spotted by a light-colored pattern on the leaf. In most cases this does not need to be addressed, but if problems do arise, an organic insecticide is usually recommended.

Grubs

Most grubs start out life as an egg laid in the ground in the fall. Over the winter, the grub digs down to protect itself from the cold, then slowly digs back to the surface in the spring, eating roots along the way. A variety of beetles comes from grubs, including the Japanese beetle. Most annual vegetables are put into the ground after the grubs have moved on to the next phase of their life. Remove grubs if you see them as you till the garden in spring.

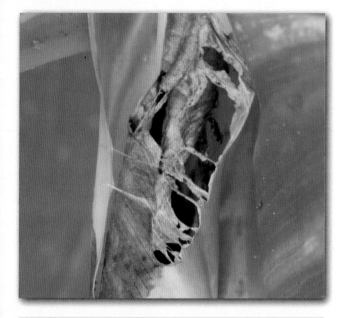

Leaf curlers

Leaf curl can be caused by several scenarios including herbicide drift, summer weather or a virus. The symptoms are the leaf edges curling downward and sometimes deforming the whole leaf. On hot, dry summer days, the natural reaction of most well-watered plants is to save water loss by closing the stomata holes on the underside of the leaf. The leaf's appearance will then return to normal in the evening when the temperature drops. Herbicide drift is most commonly seen when herbicides are applied to areas near the garden. Prompt removal of these leaves usually allows new foliage to emerge and sustain the plant. Aphid-type insects can also cause a leaf to curl by its eating pattern. In this case, the fuzzy underside of the leaf shows evidence of insect damage, which is generally restricted to just one or two leaves. Removal of these leaves removes the issue. Finally, tomatoes specifically can be affected by a virus that curls the leaf too. The pattern of leaves affected usually indicates if a virus is the cause, as the whole plant shows signs of curling and deformity in the leaves.

Scale

Scale is a hard-sided insect that gets its nutrients from the stem or leaf of the plant. The scale starts out life as an egg and progresses to a crawling insect before finally settling in one place to feed. Some scale insects produce a slick excrement that is attractive to ants, which helps show you the location of the scale. The hard "shell" of the scale makes it impenetrable to insecticides, but as the insect does require oxygen to survive, it can be smothered with oil. Most plants can cope with a minor outbreak of scale, and many birds feed on the insects, so don't be too hasty to remove these unless you have to.

Whiteflies

Whiteflies and other little flies tend to move when you brush against the plant. The colonies feed on plant juices and are able to move from one plant to another. Look under the leaf to see these little guys and, if necessary, dislodge by shaking the plant.

Molds and fungal issues

Hot humid summer weather is perfect for a host of molds and fungal activity. Large leaves of squash are particularly noted as being susceptible to downy mildew, which looks like a white film over the surface of the leaf. Cool, damp spring is another time when molds and fungus take over plants.

One of the many funguses around in the spring is damping off disease, which kills young spring seedlings. Weather-related diseases are hard to control, but a strong, healthy plant will go a long way to survival, so don't rush plants out to the ground before the conditions are ready. Cool soil in the spring as well as cool temperatures for summer vegetables are a common source of issues. For mold or fungus on just one or two leaves, take those leaves off and let the plant continue to grow normally. For more general coverage, an organic fungicide or mold treatment (be sure you know which one you have before you pick these treatments up) can be used. Fungal issues that invade the plant from the soil upward generally lead to the whole plant having to be removed. Pick resistant varieties to grow if this is a problem in your area and remember to rotate crops each season.

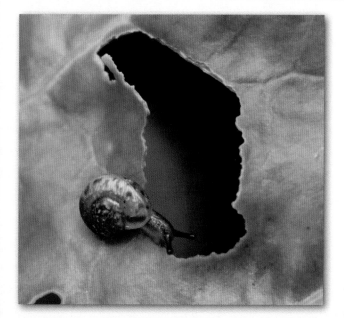

Slugs and snails

These little slippery guys come out in the moist overnight hours to feast on your vegetable leaves. Damage is seen as large holes, similar to those made by the caterpillars. Often you will see a trail of dried slime from the beast, even if you cannot find him yourself. Sprinkling diatomaceous earth, which is a sharp material that causes the slug to lacerate its belly, encourages them to go somewhere else. Sprinkle the compound around the raised bed to stop the slugs, which tend to spend the day at the very edge of the raised bed where the soil is cooler. Barriers are not overly effective, as the slug can climb into the bed from the ground or over any collar that you put around the seedling. Hot, dry weather also helps to alleviate the problem.

Rodents and animals

Rodents and animal damage is perhaps the most severe; some animals can wreak havoc overnight. For most animals, exclusion is the best remedy. Deer and groundhogs can be deterred with sturdy fencing. Some botanical sprays work for deer and many other animals (but not groundhogs). Covering the garden bed with netting helps deter the birds from feasting on your berries, and chicken wire fencing helps to keep rabbits out of the garden. ■

Types of Containers and Their Uses

Ceramic containers

Ceramic or pottery containers, if meant for growing, are usually glazed on the exterior and have a hole in the base. Matching saucers are a bonus with some smaller containers. Small, 6-8-inch pottery containers are great for indoor growing and fit easily onto a windowsill or table. Ceramic containers are usually circular rather than square in shape, and come in many colors and designs, making it possible to find one that fits into your décor. Groups of containers in bright colors look great on a deck or in the middle of a patio table. One of the advantages of larger ceramic containers, apart from color selection and overall style, is that the weight keeps them upright in all but the worst summer storms. The biggest drawback with ceramic containers is that they are breakable and tend to crack if left outside in cold winter weather.

Clay or terracotta containers

Terracotta containers have been around gardens forever. One very attractive quality is that they will take on a slightly green patina after a few years. Small and large containers are commonly found in garden centers, as well as strawberry pots, which are ideal for many other edibles besides just strawberries. Clay containers are not light, so put larger ones into position before filling them. And like ceramic containers, clay cracks if left outside in areas where cold winters are long and harsh. The clay is unglazed, which can wick the moisture from the growing medium; so, these containers need to be watched carefully, and in hot summers

watered often. When damp, the clay turns a darker shade, making this an indicator of when to water. Terracotta containers fit into a variety of landscape areas, including lining one side of steps or sitting clustered together on the patio. The classic color blends well with older homes as well as new apartment balconies.

Plastic containers

The world of plastic has made it possible to find containers in virtually any shape, size and color for a very modest price. They can be flexible, rigid, brightly colored or mimic the look of true terracotta containers. Some plastic containers do not have the hole in the bottom, so you can make holes in these if needed. Before you start drilling, look for recessed circles on the bottom. If there are any, this will be a slightly thinner plastic area that you can punch out. This is easier to do if you turn the container upside down. Using a thick nail and hammer, or by drilling with a ¼ inch bit, make a hole in the center of the base. For larger containers, such as plastic weed buckets, make several more holes around the edge of the base as well.

A plastic container with no hole in the base can be useful as a decorative cover to house a basic nursery container. Think about grouping a variety of sizes and colors together to make and attractive display. To optimize space in small areas, you can find window box designs and containers to fit onto balcony or deck railings. The main advantages of plastic containers are that they are cheap, light-

weight, come in many colors, sizes and shapes and can be found in every garden department. The down side is that the most common plastics are not recyclable and thus are not as environmentally friendly as other containers.

Coco-lined containers

These containers have a natural look. The earliest designs came with one flat side to make them look like horse or cattle hay baskets. These still work well on walls and other vertical features. The lining material is sourced from the coconut shell and is strong enough to last a season or two in the garden. Typically, the framework is black metal and has a slightly rustic look. Designs range from wall planters and hanging baskets to free-standing containers. These containers may not be suitable for root crops and tall vegetables such as tomatoes, but are perfect for salad vegetables, herbs and small vegetable varieties bred for container growing. The biggest advantage is that drainage is never an issue, and the containers have a classic, elegant look. The liner does have to be replaced most years but is quite economical and can be recycled into the compost pile.

Hypertufa containers

Hypertufa is a lightweight, concrete-like material that you can make at home or purchase. These containers have the appearance of old concrete and can be made into troughs as well as conventional, round containers. Although much lighter than concrete, they do contain about one-third concrete, making these containers quite heavy. The material is porous, but it drains better if you have a hole in the base. The containers are widely used as troughs for alpine plants, but more recently they have been used for plants, including vegetables. Making the container yourself keeps the cost down and allows you to create the exact size that you need.

Cloth containers

The problem with plastic containers is that they are not biodegradable, but fabric containers, like Smart Pots, are now on the market and have become popular because they are not only biodegradable but economical, too. The fabric can be found in basic black or attractive colors, and the sizes range from about a foot in diameter to larger ones similar in size to kiddie wading pools. They also fold down for easy storage in the winter. Like the coco liners, these cloth containers drain well. When placed on a deck or patio, the cloth "air prunes" the roots, which keeps the roots inside the container. This is particularly useful when dealing with aggressive plants like mint.

A few more container options include:

Pulp and composite materials

These containers can come in many shapes, sizes and colors, including quite large containers. The advantage of composites is that the containers look like pottery or concrete but are very light and economical. This allows you to decorate your patio with large containers big enough for beans and tomatoes while not breaking your back getting the container home.

Biodegradable containers

For something appealing to the eye, biodegradable containers are making an entrance to the market. They are appealing to the eye as well as being biodegradable. Bright, smooth-sided containers in window box or round designs are great options for those who want to change the container every few years. Color schemes go in and out of fashion in the garden (and on Madison Avenue); buying attractive containers in the latest colors allows you to be environmentally friendly and fashionable. Look for these, which are made from bamboo, at your local nursery.

Grow bags

For the simplest growing experience, you do not need a container at all. The mix that you pick up at the store can be the container! Cut an "X" in the top of the bag of potting mix, and punch a few holes in the base of the bag. Water the mix well then plant a tomato, pepper or squash seed in the "X". Keep the bag moist, not wet, and watch the plant grow. At the end of the season, empty the bag into a garden bed or compost pile. The biggest advantage of this way of growing is cost – even the cheapest container needs a soil mix for the plants to grow and using the bag as the container saves you buying another one. This is a perfect first experience for new growers. The outlay is minimal and the success rate, if the growing mix contains fertilizers, is very good. Just remember to keep the mix watered. ■

Some Natural Fertilizers and What They Do

If you are trying to stay chemical-free in your veggie garden, here is a brief look at some more natural fertilizers you may have heard about. Of course, there is that most basic of naturals, compost and compost tea, which I have written about in Chapter Three). But there are others you should be aware of, too.

Azomite

Azomite is a volcanically derived mineral that contains numerous minerals and elements. Particularly rich in phosphorus (which tomatoes enjoy), calcium, iron and magnesium. It has also been shown to provide natural immunity to plants from disease and pests.

Microbial fertilizers

These are relatively new on the market and they aim to enrich the soil around the roots with healthy microbes. Various microbes can help ward off diseases and increase overall vigor in the plant health. Microbial fertilizers come in liquid or granular forms.

Greensand

Greensand is a medium-grain mineral material that is high in potassium and iron and used primarily as a soil conditioner. Clay and sandy soils can both be improved with this mineral-rich sand but contrary to play sand, greensand does not form a concrete layer (caliche) under the surface.

Seaweed/Kelp

Seaweed is gathered from coastal areas. Since the oceans contain minerals and salts, so does the seaweed. Like alfalfa, seaweed is a great all-round source of nutrients, as well as containing growth stimulator hormones.

These four natural fertilizers are derived from field crops. These field crops all have great benefits and can provide a fertilizer that is non-animal derived. The down side is that most of the sources for the crops have been compromised with Roundup Ready genes and even after they are in the meal form, some residual RoundUp can remain, causing issues in your garden.

Alfalfa

Alfalfa is a field-grown grain from the pea family that contains a wide range of macro as well as micro nutrients. Regarded as one of the best all-round organic nutrient sources, alfalfa provides nitrogen, phosphorus and potassium for a general NPK of around 3-2-1. It is also rich in calcium and magnesium and plant hormones, which increase vigorous root and plant growth.

Canola meal

Canola is part of the mustard family and yields good amounts of nitrogen as well as minor amounts of phosphorus and potassium. It breaks down quickly in the soil for a great spring boost to crops. Canola may also be able to inhibit the germination of seeds, so take care to use it for areas of perennial vegetables or well established seedlings only.

Cottonseed meal

Cottonseed meal is derived from the seed that is inside the cotton boll. The seed is crushed to form a fine powder rich in nitrogen, phosphorus and potassium in a 6-2-2 ratio. Cottonseed meal can be used to loosen clay soil as well as bind sandy soil.

Soybean meal

Soybean meal is the residue from the soybean after the oils have been removed. Soybean is a legume that delivers nitrogen to the soil plus minor amounts of phosphorus and potassium. It can be used as a cover crop to enrich the soil over the winter. ■

RESOURCES

INDEX

ACKNOWLEDGMENTS

ABOUT THE AUTHOR

Resources

Books

All New Square Foot Gardening:
   The Revolutionary Way to Grow More in
   Less Space (2nd edition), Mel Bartholomew
   (Cool Springs Press, 2013)

The Year-Round Vegetable Gardener:
   How to Grow Your own Food 365 Days a Year,
   No Matter Where You Live, Niki Jabbour
   (Storey Publishing, 2011)

Specialty Containers

My Garden Post – vertical gardens
   (www.mygardenpost.com)

Smart Pots – fabric containers (smartpots.com)

Greenbo – Railing and fence containers
   (www.greenbo.co)

Aerogarden – hydroponic garden
   (www.aerogarden.com)

Plants

Bonnie Plants – nationwide
   (www.bonnieplants.com)

Brazelberries – container raspberries and
   blueberries (www.brazelberries.com)

Your local independent nursery

Seeds

Burpee (www.burpee.com);
   Customer service/catalogue: 1-800-888-1447

Botanical Interests (www.botanicalinterests.com);
   Customer service: 877-821-4340

Baker Creek (www.rareseeds.com);
   Customer service: 417-924-8917

Johnny's Seeds (www.johnnyseeds.com);
   Customer service: 877-564-6697

Renee's Garden Seeds (www.reneesgarden.com);
   Customer service: 1-888-880-7228

Seed Savers Exchange (www.seedsavers.org)
Customer service: 563-382-5990

Community Gardening

The American Community Gardening
   Association (www.communitygarden.org)

Index

Index

Acknowledgments

Books start out as a nugget of an idea that develops over time to something worth writing about, and I have had tremendous support from the industry in general while writing this book. I particularly want to thank four companies that supplied containers and made it possible for me to take photographs of my own produce growing: Kurt Reiger and Marty Gottlieb from Smart Pots, for supplying a range of Smart Pots for me to grow vegetables in; Marc Llona and Oliver Gardner at MyGardenPost, for introducing me to a great way to grow in a vertical system; Liron Gola at Greenbo, for sending a selection of colorful containers for the deck and fence, and Ben Gill from Aerogarden, who supplied their very user friendly hydroponic system. These innovative containers make it much easier for gardeners in small or temporary places to grow at least some of their own vegetables.

I want to thank Mel Bartholomew for his kind endorsement of this book, and for introducing me to Square Foot Gardening and making my veggie gardening life much easier.

This book could not have been produced without the encouragement and support of St. Lynn's Press, the best team out there. Paul Kelly, Publisher, who has guided the project starting from a tentative Facebook message with an idea, through to the final product; Holly Rosborough, Art Director, who guided me through the images and gave helpful photography hints along the way; and of course Cathy Dees, Senior Editor, who is the most patient and encouraging editor that I have come across. Thanks also to Chloe Wertz, Publicity, for helping me set up talks across the country.

Thanks also go to all the gardeners who welcomed me and my camera into their gardens: Camille De Santos, who grows great vegetables in containers on a pretty patio; Betty Bensen, who has an amazing garden in a very small outdoor space – her small gardens and containers line the property and are buffeted by stiff breezes, making tough conditions to grow in; Milutin Calukovic, who happily chatted to me when I knocked on the door to introduce myself; Carol Case Siracuse and Tom Palamusa, who were introduced to me via Facebook and shared with me their experience growing on a garage roof.

From the next generation of gardeners I want to thank Asher Wittenberg, who found that sending his mother an image on Facebook got it circulated by the proud Mama; it caught my eye and he was gracious enough to chat with me about

his first gardening experience. And our own son, Jonathan, who asked me to help him put in his first 4x4 garden this past spring. Both these guys have grown up with their mothers gardening and are now on their own with their first gardens.

These people illustrate that gardeners are such friendly people, and true gardeners always find a place to grow a few vegetables.

A big hug goes to Doug Oster, who prodded me for months to get in touch with St. Lynn's Press and was my biggest cheerleader when I signed the contract. Doug is one of the many wonderful garden friends who supported and were enthusiastic when they heard I was doing this book – so thanks to you all!

Finally, I want to thank my husband, who, newly retired, never fussed about me being shut away in the study working; and the kids – Jonathan, Christopher, Nathan and Antony – who are now making their way in the world and hopefully will always find a place to grow a few veg for themselves wherever they are.

About the Author

KATE COPSEY grew up in England, where vegetables were always part of the family garden. Since then, she has grown vegetables in many ways and many regions of the U.S. – in a variety of gardens both large and small. She and her husband recently downsized from five acres in the Midwest to under one acre in urban New Jersey.

In 1998 she certified as a Master Gardener in Virginia. She has kept her Master Gardener certification status active as her family relocated through several states. Kate was the first host of the popular America's Home Grown Veggie Show and continued as host for over six years with the program. She was a national board member for The Herb Society of America and is currently on the board of The Garden Writers Association.

Kate's writing has appeared in local, regional and international newspapers, as well as a number of garden and lifestyle magazines. She enjoys giving presentations to the public and has been a popular speaker wherever she has lived. Her talks range from basic gardening to herbs and vegetables – including those essentials of downsized garden living: growing vegetables in containers and raised beds.

www.katecopsey.com

OTHER BOOKS FROM ST. LYNN'S PRESS

www.stlynnspress.com

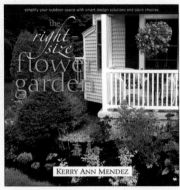

The Right-Size Flower Garden
by Kerry Mendez
160 pages • Hardback
ISBN: 978-0-9892688-7-5

Plants with Benefits
by Helen Yoest
160 pages, Hardback
ISBN: 978-0-9892688-0-6

The 20-30 Something Garden Guide
by Dee Nash
160 pages, Hardback
ISBN: 978-0-9855622-7-4

A Garden to Dye For
by Chris McLaughlin
160 pages, Hardback
ISBN: 978-0-9855622-8-1